SO-BDO-941

PRAISE FOR
WORK, YOUR WAY

"The consultant's playbook. The practical guide to consulting with tangible exercises and best practices."

—CINDY DAVIDSON,
Executive Communications Consultant

"A must-read for anyone considering a career in consulting. Lisa shares her tried-and-true recipe for success in this practical consulting playbook. You will learn from one of the best!"

—BETH R. CHASE,
Founder and CEO, c3/consulting

"Coaching and consulting both started the twenty-first century with somewhat fixed images (one colorful with a whistle and tennis shoes, the other colorless in a gray flannel suit). In the years since, both have emerged as renewed and now essential gears for our culture's productivity engine. In *Work, Your Way*, Lisa (who is a rare combination of visionary leader and hands-on entrepreneur) explains the components—from personal attitude and life balance to personal branding and connection—of how to consistently succeed in finding, contracting with, and delighting clients. 'Mastery, purpose, and freedom' are the things I wish for every leader I work with. And, in *Work, Your Way*, Lisa explains how to achieve each of those things. If you long to bring consistently great service to your clients, this book will show you how. With compelling stories, she underscores the challenges and benefits of participation in the gig economy. For this moment in history, Lisa's timing is spot-on."

—PATRICIA BURGIN, MA MCC,
Founder and CEO, SeattleCoach,
and Author of *The Essential Coaching Leader*

"I have hired many consultants as a former Microsoft executive and valued the ones who added instant expertise and integrated seamlessly into my team. I have observed firsthand how Lisa's approach helps consultants understand how to stand out in a crowded marketplace and deliver excellence in generating constant referrals. It's a must-read for anyone choosing consulting as a career."

—RICK WONG,
Former Vice President, Microsoft, and Author
of *Winning Lifelong Customers with The Five Abilities*

"*Work, Your Way* is the how-to guide working parents have been waiting for! The shift that Lisa describes in the book makes you take a step back and ask yourself, 'Is this career I've worked so hard for actually worth it?' Lisa helps us define who we are, what we want to achieve, and how we can design our career to align with the life we want for ourselves and our families. As Lisa states, and I have also always believed, consulting is the future of work—so it's time to take the leap and embrace the incredible upside that comes with being the CEO of your career."

—SARAH DUENWALD,
Coauthor of *Back to Business* and
Cofounder and Head of Operations, The Swing Shift:
The Destination for Women in Career Transition

"This book provides crucial guidance for professionals seeking to become part of a fundamental shift in the labor force to independence and entrepreneurial service. We only get one shot at creating a life, and people who are dissatisfied with the daily corporate grind will benefit immensely from the roadmap provided by this book toward a more fulfilling life in consulting. Opportunity awaits those willing to take the plunge to control their own work lives. Readers won't find anyone with greater insights about this journey than Lisa."

—SCOTT DAWSON,
Dean at University of Colorado, Denver

"This book is so overdue—Lisa has a way of translating years of experience and wisdom into brilliant, practical, actionable direction everyone can benefit from. Bravo!"

—JANE BOULWARE,
Board Member and C-Level Executive

"The future of work is now upon us—but Lisa was there first. She's been an inspiration to my students not just for her vision but for her fiercely independent entrepreneurialism. Now, *Work, Your Way* is at the top of my list for anyone who wants to own the freedom and flexibility of their professional future. Oh, and as a consultant myself, I learned a lot too!"

—HANSON HOSEIN,
Cofounder, Communication Leadership
graduate program at the University of Washington,
and President, HRH Media Group LLC

"If you're stuck in a corporate job and looking for an alternative, *Work, Your Way* is a must-read. Lisa writes from personal experience and from the heart, providing not only encouragement but also a practical and complete guide on how to set up your consulting business. Start your transformation journey with this book in hand!"

—CHARLENE LI,
New York Times Bestselling Author of
The Disruption Mindset and Founder and
Senior Fellow, Altimeter, a Prophet company

"As an executive, I know that bringing in the right consultants to drive critical projects was 'make or break' for my project, my team, my company, and myself. Lisa's book is a practical and inspirational guide for corporate professionals who choose consulting and want to be great. This book will help you learn how to be the kind of consultant whom executives love to hire and return to again and again—the kind that 'make it' for their clients."

—ELISSA FINK,
Board Member and
Former CMO, Tableau Software

"Work can be delicious, energizing, filling you with all the feels you hope for . . . and the key ingredient is intention. Lisa lays out how to move from intention to execution in this substantive playbook on how to work on terms that work for your full life. Holistic working and living is now a nonnegotiable. This is your guide to make it happen. I'm buying this for all our consultants."

—SALLY THORNTON,
Founder and CEO, Forshay Inc.

LISA HUFFORD

WORK, *YOUR* WAY

REINVENT YOURSELF, CREATE THE LIFE YOU WANT, AND THRIVE AS A CONSULTANT

HarperCollins
Leadership

An Imprint of HarperCollins

*To Jack and Ian, who continue to be my
greatest inspiration, teachers, and purpose*

Published by HarperCollins Leadership, an imprint of HarperCollins Focus LLC.

Any internet addresses, phone numbers, or company or product information printed in this book are offered as a resource and are not intended in any way to be or to imply an endorsement by HarperCollins Leadership, nor does HarperCollins Leadership vouch for the existence, content, or services of these sites, phone numbers, companies, or products beyond the life of this book.

ISBN 978-1-4002-2106-6 (eBook)
ISBN 978-1-4002-2104-2 (PBK)

Library of Congress Control Number: 2021937234

Printed in the United States of America
21 22 23 24 25 LSC 10 9 8 7 6 5 4 3 2 1

CONTENTS

ACKNOWLEDGMENTS

IT TAKES A VILLAGE TO write a book, and I am deeply grateful to so many people who supported me and helped to bring these ideas and concepts to life.

My parents: Thank you for telling me I could do whatever I put my mind to and for supporting any interest I had, from 4-H to cheerleading at an early age. You are both lifelong teachers and gave me the space and support to always dream big.

David: Thank you for providing an endless ocean of support and encouragement that gives me the confidence to take risks in my career. I am grateful that you allow me to be my creative, idea-generating, entrepreneurial self.

Jack and Ian: You are the reason I decided that my career ladder was on the wrong wall. Thank you for teaching me patience and purpose. I became a consultant because I wanted to have the time and ability to show you the world, and every year I am grateful to be able to do that with you.

Consultants: Thank you to the thousands of consultants who have trusted me to guide, support, and inspire them over the years and have given me the credibility to share the learning in this book. To each of the long-term consultants who generously shared their stories, I am beyond grateful. They include Alice, Cassondra, Hai, Christopher, Heidi, Kate, Catharine, Krissi, Allison, Deanna, Keri, Young, Rupali, and Sydney. Your stories show us we are not alone on this journey, and we are more alike than different.

Clients: Thank you for your partnership and hiring us to help you achieve your goals. You have provided the opportunity for consultants to do the work they love.

Stephanie Chacharon: Thank you for agreeing to help me bring this book to life with your passion for writing. You are a natural project manager, and your attention to detail helped me stay on track. I appreciate you helping me structure and edit my teaching points and weave in the consultant stories for a richer reader experience.

Simplicity Consulting staff: Thank you to Carrie Morris and Cheryl Kolodzaike. Without your day-to-day support of the business, I would not have been able to sequester myself to finish this book. Your dedication and commitment are unparalleled, and I appreciate you, our staff, and consultants who make a difference in so many people's lives every day.

AJ Harper and Laura Stone: Thank you for teaching me how to write a top three book. I am grateful for your teachings and developmental edits and for the writers group comments that made the book better. I appreciate AJ teaching me to write a book for someone, not about something. Mitch Shepard: Thank you for recommending that I join AJ Harper's workshop.

Ali Spain, executive director of the Microsoft Alumni Network: Thank you for recommending me as an author to the HarperCollins Leadership editorial team. I am proud to be included as an author representing the Microsoft Alumni and HCL partnership.

Sara Kendrick: Thank you for your partnership and flexibility with the book-writing process. You have been a joy to work with.

Winston, my Cavalier King Charles Spaniel: Thank you for your emotional support during the book-writing process. You inspired me to go on long walks where I could think through concepts, and your lap-sitting as I wrote most of the book provided grounding.

INTRODUCTION

WE ALL HAVE THAT LIGHTBULB moment.

Maybe you've had it and you're gathering the resolve to act. Or maybe it stopped you in your tracks, and you felt your life change in an instant. Or maybe it hasn't happened yet, but you're starting to feel a shift within yourself. Wherever you are in your life right now, I hope this book serves as your lightbulb moment. Whatever caused you to pick up this book, I'm glad you're here.

You already have everything you need to do the work you love and create the life you want. You might be thinking: *What the heck is she talking about? She doesn't know me. I don't see how this is possible.* You wouldn't be the first person who's told me that. Many of the thousands of professionals I have advised since 2007 have thought the same. And in every conversation, whenever they shared their doubts, I would take them through the same exercises included in this book to remind them of their greatness.

We all have unique talents and gifts. You, too, have greatness. We lose sight of it sometimes and need a reminder. I wrote this book to help you recognize your strengths, spark that lightbulb moment, boost your confidence, and set you on a path of action. Action doesn't have to be hard. This is going to be a fun journey! Together, we'll discover your personal brand, identify the work you love to do right now, explore how to do more of the work that lights you up, and, ultimately, create a life with meaning and purpose. Isn't that what we all want?

Here's my promise to you. No matter your background or current situation, you already have everything you need to do the work you love, and I will show you how. As you venture through this book, I am right here beside you to provide support, encouragement, and guide you back to yourself. You can gain control of your work and your life on your terms. We'll get there together.

Don't worry if you got lost somewhere along the way. It happens to the best of us, especially corporate professionals. Each person chooses to do consulting for his or her own reasons, whether it's burnout, desire to do the work you love, or to own your life. I've heard it all from countless people who have sat across from me, asking for advice and guidance. I will share the same advice with you that I have shared with them; you always have options.

Take Keri, a corporate professional turned marketing strategist for startups. When I asked her at what point in her career she chose consulting, she shared the story of her father's sudden death.

"He wasn't sick, and we weren't expecting it. I remember being at the funeral home and stepping outside for a team call because we were launching this huge program, and I needed to coordinate all the global resources," she said, shaking her head. "It was crazy, but that was my job."

Then came time to choose the words to etch into his headstone.

"You want it to be 'great dad' or 'great friend.' I just had this gut feeling that, truly at this point, mine would read 'she finished projects on time and on budget,'" Keri told me. "I had this moment of *what am I doing*? All the things that I know in my heart are most important to me are getting the least of my attention."

She gave notice the next week.

Keri started to think about the opportunity cost of her work. She didn't want to just show up and spend time on tasks. That didn't fulfill her needs anymore. She wanted either to be doing something with impact or to be with her young kids. And the opportunity cost of her career had grown too steep to ignore.

"I felt very clearly that my purpose was not what I'd been doing," she said. "I needed something where I didn't have that opportunity cost. It was going to have to be something bigger and different."

Consulting is Keri's "something bigger and different." It provides the flexibility and variety that top Keri's list of nonnegotiables. The variety fuels the builder in Keri. She's able to do the work she loves in a way that works for her life.

"I can't say I actually work less, but it's fluid enough that I can show up for all the things that are important to me," she added. "I can finally plan my work around my life instead of planning my life around my work. That's a game changer for me."

Maybe, like Keri, you've been rocked by the startling realization that your priorities are out of balance and you need to find another option. Maybe you've felt the opportunity cost of working within a rigid or cutthroat structure that constantly demands more from you. Maybe you dream of redesigning your life around what's most important to you, not what you've always believed you should do. If so, you are not alone. I was there, too, and I reached a point in my career where I needed to find another option. After more than a decade in a successful corporate career, I was searching for a way to better integrate work into my life. For me, as it was for Keri, that other option was consulting.

Ever since I set out on my own as a consultant in 2006, I've received meeting requests from professionals asking how consulting works, mostly by women with a story similar to my own. I didn't intend to become known as the woman who successfully left her corporate job to consult, but I quickly recognized that I was in a unique position to help others. They wanted to learn how they could transition from their corporate role to consulting. They wanted to do the work they loved on their terms without having to compete for the next level. They wanted the flexibility to juggle meaningful work with other demands such as motherhood. They wanted the freedom to own their work and their lives.

Those meetings became more frequent, and I was happy to share my learnings and pointers for landing contracts. I was repeatedly asked the same questions. People wanted to know how to find a client, set the right rate, get referrals, and ultimately determine if consulting was right for them. I had been there, and I had answers.

Those one-on-one conversations soon turned into a free Consulting 101 class that I taught every Tuesday in a small conference room in downtown Kirkland, Washington. Each week, I'd share my insights with twenty-some people, all wanting to find meaningful work, freedom, and flexibility. By then, I had established an S corporation, Simplicity Consulting, and I was the sole employee.

Then something unexpected happened. Some of those same people started coming back. "I took your advice, and I have a contract," they'd say. "Can I bill my project through your company?"

That's when I realized that Simplicity Consulting had the potential to be bigger than me. I was already noticing other talented professionals wanting the same lifestyle that I had created, and I was inspired to help them make it happen for themselves and create a unique company.

So, I took another leap. I stopped taking my own projects and started exclusively providing those early consultants with a back office, invoicing, and coaching support while they were working on their contracts. I wanted to create the company that hadn't existed when I set out on my own—a supportive culture of professionals making a living doing great work, backed by a company with transparent and trustworthy values. My vision was, and still is, to help people thrive in the new world of work. I continue to feel called to help professionals rediscover the work they love, because work is so much of our lives. If I can help people feel great about their work, it cascades to all areas of their lives.

Beginning in 2009, Simplicity Consulting was honored to be named to the Inc. 5000 (a list of the fastest-growing, privately held companies in the United States) for five consecutive years. We've been recognized as a best place to work and one of the largest woman-owned private companies in Washington State. We continue to provide enterprise marketing services to the Pacific Northwest's most innovative companies and grow by referrals and word of mouth from our loyal clients and consultants.

In 2013, I was struck by this *Forbes* quote: "By the year 2020, 40 percent of US workers won't want to be your employee." That is when I recognized that changes in the future landscape of work were accelerating. I envisioned managers needing a new playbook for how to access and manage external talent and create blended teams. I wrote *Navigating the Talent Shift* in 2016 as the definitive guide for managers to build on-demand teams that drive innovation, control costs, and get results. The book includes my SPEED methodology—a practical, actionable strategy for building on-demand teams—that we use every day at Simplicity Consulting with our clients.[1]

While I've advised business leaders from a host of companies and industries, I've never stopped focusing on the other side of the equation: you, the talent. Even today, fourteen years later and counting, my inbox is full of information requests. The through line, from successful professionals with long corporate careers to recent college graduates, is that they're all in search of the same thing. They want the freedom to own their work and life. They want options.

This book is everything I know about how to create and land contract work and successfully design your life by choosing contract work. It is a viable alternative to traditional full-time employment for white-collar professionals. Like me, the successful consultants I feature in the pages of this book have built the plane while in flight and learned what to do and not to do along the way. There is no governing body, no school of consulting, no rulebook—until now. You are holding the ultimate guide that will show you how to do it for yourself.

Work consumes most of our thoughts and waking hours. It influences every aspect of our lives: relationships, self-confidence, financial stability, and mental health. Yet fulfillment can be elusive. Did you know that 66 percent of people aren't fulfilled at work?[2] That's two-thirds of the workforce showing up unfulfilled, unhappy, and not bringing their best contributions to the world. It doesn't have to be that way.

In his bestselling book *Drive: The Surprising Truth About What Motivates Us*, Daniel Pink says that ideal work is about autonomy, mastery, and purpose.[3] When I read that definition, I thought, *That's consulting!*

So why don't more people seek it out? Do they not know how? Do they not believe that it's possible to love their work?

Since the start of my own company, I have talked with many people who were not happy in their jobs but stayed put, often for years, complaining all the while. Don't be that person. It's no way to live. It will make you miserable and often everyone else around you, too. There is a place for you, and it is up to you to find it. There is something better out there. You can find work that you excel at that also brings you joy. But you must be intentional about it.

I am passionate about helping professionals recognize that contract work is a viable and fulfilling alternative to traditional employment. You can do the work you love however you love to do it and realize success at work *and* life. Each of us has the opportunity to create a positive ripple effect in the lives of those around us. Work is critical to our dignity, self-worth, and livelihood, and when we find success at work, we tend to find success in other areas of our lives. Find your fulfillment, and you and the people you love will be better for it. Your fulfillment will inspire others.

It's not just theory or squishy sentiments. I have seen this play out in the lives of thousands of professionals who have walked through the doors at Simplicity Consulting. They've taken the same guidance that you are reading in this book, done the work, and have intentionally created a life that is fulfilling to them. And they keep going, delivering great work and building their portfolio with each project.

I never expected this story would be mine, and yet it is one that has led me down a path of purpose and fulfillment to help others. It is the story of how I became an accidental consultant, entrepreneur, and teacher. I have two sons to thank for showing me what is most important and motivating me to choose this path. I'm inspired to help put you on your path to success.

Have you had your lightbulb moment yet? Are you ready to take control of your destiny? Choose yourself, and let's get going.

PART I
The Future of Work and You

ONE

CHANGE CREATES OPTIONS

*"If you change the way you look at things,
the things you look at change."*
—WAYNE DYER

I NEVER SAW IT COMING.

Early on a weekday morning, the plane descended into John Wayne Airport. The pressure of my breast milk built until it was ready to erupt like a volcano all down the front of my pressed white collared shirt. All I could think about was racing off the plane and into the nearest bathroom, preferably one with a little privacy and an outlet.

I hurried to deplane, the gigantic black breast pump case thrown over one shoulder and a black briefcase over the other. In the terminal, I got settled in a bathroom stall and plugged in the pump. (Airport nursing pods were unimaginable in 2004.) As I perched on an unsanitary airport toilet seat and pumped breast milk for my son, Jack, who was miles away at home in Seattle with his nanny, I thought about how crazy and unsustainable my life had become, juggling work and motherhood. Is this really what having it all looked like?

But I didn't have much time to reflect. I had to finish pumping, rent a car, and arrive at my customer's site in an hour to deliver a high-stakes presentation. Off I went—just like I had every day since I started working in Corporate America in 1993—except that day I began to feel a shift inside myself. A shift I didn't see coming.

The part of me that wanted to climb the career ladder was starting to be eclipsed by the part of me that wanted to be present and engaged with my son. That shift was scary. I'd always worked hard, and I'd been rewarded for it. Now, with a baby and a career vying for my time and energy, I wasn't feeling successful at work or home. But what else could I do? I knew that the stay-at-home-mom life wasn't for me. Was there another option?

I have always loved working. Nothing is more fun to me than helping customers solve problems and manage partnerships. I have been grateful to work for amazing corporations where I learned every day from smart people doing important work.

Jack, my first son, was born in 2003. I kept up the pace of my work, though I knew it wasn't sustainable. At that time, there weren't many women, especially mothers, in executive corporate leadership roles. And I saw executives earning a lot of money, but often at the expense of their personal health and their families.

In the following days and months, that little shift I had felt in the airport bathroom became a constant thought pattern. That recognition of just how hard it is to juggle work and family. That pull of wanting to be a professional, and wanting to be with my kids, and wanting to not feel guilty in either moment. Something had changed in me. I realized it was my definition of success.

By 2005, I was pregnant again and exhausted. I took stock of where I was: stretched thin and laden with mommy guilt. Suddenly, I was back in that airport bathroom, frantically pumping before rushing off to a client meeting. How could I possibly do this with two?

Is my proverbial career ladder on the wrong wall? I wondered. I'd spent thirteen years of blood, sweat, and tears building a credible sales career and overseeing the strategic direction for huge, multinational partner engagements, and now I was questioning whether to quit my job to be a stay-at-home mom.

The only pace I knew was 100 mph. I needed to find something that was not that, but I didn't yet know what it was. All I knew was that I wanted to use my experience to do great work that also gave me the flexibility to be present for my soon-to-be-two young boys.

When I went on maternity leave after the arrival of Ian, my second son, in February 2006, I knew I needed to figure out what was next for me. My team had to backfill my role because it couldn't sit open for six months, and the new vice president assured me that we'd find the right job for me when I returned.

Becoming a mother set me on my path of purpose. If not for my boys, I wouldn't have had the motivation or the reason to step away from my all-consuming career. I wanted to create a life for them. I wanted to be able to show them the world. And I knew that if I didn't change course, I'd wake up one day and it would all be over, and I'd have missed out on moments I would never get back. I desperately wanted to create a path for myself that provided freedom and flexibility.

Between endless feedings, diapers, and naps, I searched for part-time or job-share roles, anything that would allow me to continue contributing and allow flexibility but not require travel. Sadly,

I couldn't find anything within my search parameters. So, I expanded them. I talked to anyone who had a job I perceived as flexible, from realtors and mortgage lenders to multilevel marketing leaders. I was open to anything. I wanted to find a way to leverage my professional experience and expertise, but none of these other career paths appealed to me beyond the flexibility. I felt like my only choices were either return to my previous role, outsource childcare, progress to the next level in my career (which would require long hours and plenty of travel), or quit and stay home with my kids. Neither option was right for me at the time. I needed to create another option.

We all need options, now more than ever.

In my work, I have met thousands of professionals who are looking for an alternative career option. Though their circumstances and life experiences vary greatly, I hear a common refrain: "I never saw it coming." It could be that they were laid off or fired. Maybe the promotion they worked toward for years never materialized. Perhaps they had to quit their job to care for a child or aging parent. Maybe they'd always dreamed of climbing the corporate ladder but ended up stressed, burned out, and in search of another option. Life happens. You can't predict what's around the corner and how it will affect your career and income.

As I write this book in the summer of 2020, we are in the throes of a global pandemic that has caught the world off guard. COVID-19 has hit every industry, every economy, and every person's way of life. The future of work is officially here, and the pandemic has accelerated it. According to *Entrepreneur* magazine, "No doubt about it, the way we work has changed dramatically, and we need to change with it. Before the pandemic, we may have thought that innovations like artificial intelligence and working remotely were things of the future.

Look around you—the future of work is here, and the transformation is continuing to accelerate."[1]

Future of work? you may be thinking. *What does that really mean and how does it affect me?* You may not see opportunity now, but I am here to tell you that it is there. Shift your perspective. Open yourself to the possibility that there is more than your current definition of work and success. I hope that once you learn about the global trends impacting business and talent, you will see opportunity for yourself in new and different ways—like I did. I experienced this shift—it opened a whole new world for me and fundamentally changed my relationship with work. As my life evolves, so does my definition of success. The future of work—that is, the transformation of work—enabled me to step into this life. It can do the same for you.

After all, over the course of a fifty-year career, the average person clocks 92,100 hours at work.[2] We spend a huge portion of our lives working, so it's no wonder we want to make it count. I wrote this book to help you close the door on a rigid career path that may no longer be serving you, and instead chart a path to greater meaning and purpose.

In times of great uncertainty and change, I remind myself that I have a choice. I can choose fear, or I can choose opportunity. I invite you to join me in the pursuit of opportunity. This book will give you the tools to forge a new path in the future of work. It will introduce you to a viable alternative to how you've traditionally viewed work. It will help you create and land a contract doing the work you love, and successfully do it again and again. It will help you articulate and achieve your own personal definition of success, not the one-size-fits-all definition that's been impressed upon you.

In this chapter, we will look at where we are today, where we are going, and, most important, what all this means for you.

The Future of Work Is Here

Future of work means many things to many people, but I'm partial to this characterization by Deloitte:

> Two powerful forces are shaping the future of work: the growing adoption of artificial intelligence in the workplace, and the expansion of the workforce to include both on- and off-balance-sheet talent.[3]

For the purposes of this book, we'll focus on that second force: talent.

Traditionally, talent has been a balance sheet item and considered overhead and a fixed cost that impacts a public company's earnings per share. But more and more companies are moving talent off the balance sheet and hiring external talent because these variable-cost resources provide the ultimate flexibility to manage expenses and limit employment risks.

Of the 57 million people in the United States who freelanced in 2018, half said that *no amount of money* would get them to take a traditional job. And many are seasoned experts: 64 percent of top professionals are opting for independent work, reports Upwork, a leading freelance platform.[4]

Fortunately for you and me, it's not just talent who wants to work this way. Nearly 60 percent of hiring managers plan to use "some form of flexible talent" in 2020, and three in four organizations have growth-limiting skills gaps.[5] Toptal, a global network of top freelancers, notes that 76 percent of organizations expect to increase their use of external talent.[6]

I often talk to leaders who are unaware of their talent options. I recently spoke with Gary, the CEO of a mid-sized company who wasn't seeing the return on investment (ROI) and business impact with his team's digital marketing efforts. His vice president of marketing had great traditional product-marketing skills, he explained to me, but lacked current digital marketing expertise. He had burned through four agencies over the last few years, spending thousands of dollars with no meaningful results. His frustration was palpable.

Just like Gary, many leaders are unaware of an alternative approach to hiring. They still try to achieve their goals by either hiring an employee or an agency. The advice I shared with Gary expanded his perspective and showed him how he could build a dynamic team. Fixed teams are the traditional, pyramid-shaped organizations where employees advance in a linear fashion based on tenure. Dynamic teams assemble a diverse group of people working on projects, a mixture of internal talent and specialized external talent.

Gary is an all-too-common example of a leader who needs a subject-matter expert to help him solve an important business challenge. That is where you come in as an expert. Leaders don't always need to create headcount and recruit for a traditional employee, they just need the right expert to help them deliver on a specific area of expertise. Leaders have all sorts of business challenges and the great consultants help them solve their problems and add immediate value.

The traditional, full-time-employee model will always exist on some level, but it assumes that employees will stick around long-term, and the policies and processes at most companies still support that premise. In reality, the average employee only stays with a company for less than five years (even less for millennials).[7] Nowadays, leaders are often better served carving out projects, like a surgeon with a scalpel, with outside experts rather than hiring fully burdened employees.

I predict that companies will increasingly move toward smaller core teams of employees and increase their access to on-demand talent and dynamic teams. Businesses can respond to change in a more agile way than the traditional hiring process, which takes months and is expensive. Managers can translate goals into projects, identify key skills and gaps, and bring in experts to add a fresh perspective, fill expertise gaps, and up-level their teams. When managers feel stuck with the team they have, I like to help them see that they can have the team they want by intentionally identifying what's missing and creating projects in which external experts can contribute to solutions.

This is where *you* come in as the expert.

Traditional Hiring Is Broken

Here's why the traditional human resources approach falls short in the new world of work.

It's too slow. According to LinkedIn, only 30 percent of companies are able to fill a vacant role within thirty days, and those who do take as long as one to four months to process a new hire.[8] In contrast, an on-demand expert can quickly be selected, hired—often in a matter of days—dropped in like a Navy Seal with a targeted mission, and add value.[9]

It's too expensive. The opportunity cost of waiting to hire the "perfect" person is enormous. It costs 213 percent of an annual salary to replace a highly skilled employee.[10] Many hiring managers search for months for the elusive unicorn who possesses every skill listed in the job description, only to see that unicorn leave for greener pastures in a year or two.

It's inflexible. Companies must be able to flex and respond to the accelerated pace of business today in order to stay relevant. Although digital transformation means something different to every company, it's evident that many companies need different skills at different times. It's incredibly hard to foresee headcount needs because business goals are changing quickly, as are the skills needed to achieve these goals.

It's focused on attrition. I recently met with a colleague who's a partner and thirty-year veteran at a large global firm. He shared with me that he observed a trend with their recent college hires who left in droves after two years or so. "How do we improve employee retention?" he asked.

I immediately thought that he was asking the wrong question, because talent has changed how they view employment with one company.

Millennials (people born in the 1980s or 1990s) and Generation Zs (those born in the late 1990s and early 2000s) view work in a new way. Unlike their predecessors, millennials don't perceive loyalty as staying somewhere for a long time. They see an employer as an opportunity to learn, advance, build skills, add value, and then move on to a new opportunity where they can learn more or advance faster. It's not bad; it's just different. Corporations shouldn't be surprised when they lose their younger talent. They need to understand how different generations are showing up at work and adapt their hiring practices to meet talent's new expectations.

Generational Approaches to Work

Social and economic factors shape the soul of each generation, contributing to distinct differences when it comes to work. While we must be careful not to generalize for all people within a group, it's important to understand how these generational perspectives influence the current landscape.

Let's start with millennials. According to *Inc.*, they'll compose 75 percent of the global workforce by 2025, and they already compose more than two-thirds of the employee base at innovative companies like Ernst & Young and Accenture.[11] Their attitudes are dramatically shifting traditional employment. As digital natives, technology shaped their lives from an early age. They value freedom and flexibility and seek purpose and meaning in their work. They are optimistic, seek mentors, desire to develop their strengths, and work collaboratively. They work "with," not "for" companies.

The millennial mentality contrasts starkly with baby boomers, who were born after World War II (1946–1964). Their careers were defined by their employers, and job security was paramount. Their work experience was highly structured with defined roles and devoid of technology. Generally, men worked nine to five, and women stayed home to raise the family.

Then there's my generation: Generation X. We want work-life balance, and we're competitive, loyal, and individualistic. Born between 1965 and 1980, we started our careers at the dawn of the internet and email. We base our view of the employee-employer relationship on these learned truths: Get a good job for a big company, work hard, do what you're told, and your manager will take care of you. I call us the *sandwich generation*, because we are sandwiched between the boomers' traditional way of working and the millennials' collaborative and flexible approach to work.

Now Gen Zs are entering the workforce. They've only known a digital world, and technology informs every aspect of their lives. They are more racially and ethnically diverse than any previous generation. They value stability and security, yet they're coming of age during a global pandemic, growing concerns over climate change, and demonstrations for racial justice. They want opportunities for advancement and the ability to create their own careers. Gen Zs' views will continue to inform and shape how companies acquire and retain talent.

Each generation has distinct preferences about how they view work and life, and companies must continue to adapt to the changing landscape.

Change, Digital Disruption, and the COVID-19 Effect

COVID-19 has cemented the arrival of the future of work and accelerated disruptive technologies. In May 2020, Microsoft CEO Satya Nadella, quantified it by saying, "We've seen two years' worth of digital transformation in two months."[12] This statement from Satya really struck me. Because of our global health crisis, innovation and creativity have skyrocketed and upended the status quo overnight. Companies were already going through digital transformation at their own pace, but COVID-19 required companies to speed up their digital efforts remotely or risk business failure.

Everything is now virtual: work, school, events, late-night TV, even graduations, birthdays, memorials, and baby showers. A few weeks of stay-home orders cured our collective aversion to video calls. Cloud-based communication and collaboration tools such as Zoom, Slack, Microsoft Teams, Google Meet and Google Chat (both of which replaced Google Hangouts), and Microsoft 365 are the lifeblood of our distributed teams and families. Remote work used to be a nice-to-have. Now, in the time of coronavirus, everyone is doing it whether they want to or not. Ready or not, companies of all sizes and types have been forced to adapt to a new way of working seemingly overnight. This new way of life happened suddenly, and we never saw it coming.

Even before the pandemic, remote work was on the rise. Disruptive technologies are enabling us to work from anywhere, changing consumer expectations and creating new business models.[13] The pace of business demands a new level of corporate agility and an overhaul of how we think about work. One thing is clear: We are not going back to the way we used to work. Companies like Twitter, Facebook, and Google have fully embraced the remote work revolution by allowing their employees to work remotely indefinitely.[14]

And if digital transformation and a pandemic weren't enough for companies to adapt to, racial injustice has become another paramount issue impacting the workplace. The murders of Ahmaud Aubrey, Breonna Taylor, and George Floyd were catalysts for protests that called for a change in 2020.[15] Institutional racism has permeated every facet of society for hundreds of years, including employment. A survey by Glassdoor found 43 percent of US employees have seen or experienced racism at work. More than half (55 percent) said their company should do more to increase diversity. Specifically, Black people reported a 60 percent higher rate of discrimination compared to whites. The spotlight now shines on racial injustice. This, too, will change the way we work. In 2020, companies historically silent on the topic have stood strong against racism. The racial justice movement has become more than a moment, and as a result diversity and inclusion will be a necessary part of the new world of work.

The new world of work is different, and it's still in transition. We have an opportunity to make it better. I predict that when COVID-

19 is under control, most people will blend working from home and the office in a more flexible way. Upwork reports that once the pandemic subsides, 62 percent of organizations plan to be more remote, and 24 percent of workers want to work from home more or exclusively.[16] And workplaces will be more diverse and inclusive.

Change is constant. In the midst of massive disruption, you have an opportunity to redefine your relationship with work. Focus on what you can control and create options for yourself.

In Search of a Viable Option

I evaluated many different careers during my maternity leave with my second son, but nothing felt right until a colleague suggested consulting. *Consulting?* I completely discounted it at first. In my head, I didn't fit the consultant profile: A man in a suit, working for a big firm, and charging top dollar for lofty strategy presentations. I had a whole narrative about why it wouldn't work for me and how I didn't fit into that image and besides, why would anyone hire me? What did I know about consulting, anyway?

But still, I was curious. Something about the idea of consulting clicked with me. I could continue to work with people I had relationships with and leverage my many years of experience. I loved rolling up my sleeves and doing the work. I thrived on helping others and making them look great. And I could work in a flexible way and own my schedule. *Could I be a consultant?* Maybe I could be a different kind of consultant than what my perceived image was. I began to think more seriously about this new way of working. It consumed my thoughts.

Was it possible to do the work I loved on a contract basis? Could I choose the clients I wanted to work for? Could I set my hours and work where and how I wanted? Could I monetize all my hard-earned experience and knowledge?

There were no guarantees, and I had a laundry list of misgivings. I might fail. I was concerned about letting go of my career and a steady paycheck. And I couldn't emulate any female role models who had chosen this path—there weren't any. But I had to take the leap.

Let me say that I was and am grateful to have a supportive husband with a dependable job who provided comfortably for our family. That added sense of security helped me take the risk. Worst-case scenario, I figured, I could always go back to a corporate job if consulting didn't work out for me, even though there was no guarantee of a job waiting for me.

So, I outlined a one-page project proposal—standing up a new revenue stream for a sales channel—that I knew was a priority for my leadership team but hadn't been worked on yet. I planned to pitch it to Sam, the vice president of the company where I was working, when we met at the end of my maternity leave to discuss my next role. On the day of our meeting, I was so nervous my stomach was doing backflips. This was my opportunity, but my insecurities and doubts came flooding in.

What will he say? Will he laugh or kick me out of his office in anger? This could be the most disastrous decision of my career. Who quits a high-paying sales director role at the world's largest software company to do contract work? And I'm pinning all my hope on consulting, something I've never even done before. Who was I to think I could do this?

I'm still not sure what gave me the confidence. Maybe I was so sleep deprived from having a baby and a toddler that I was unable to think about what would happen if it backfired. I pushed aside the negative self-talk. I was determined to find a way to juggle work and motherhood on my terms and willing to try anything that seemed to offer freedom and flexibility.

There, in Sam's office, I started by expressing how much I had loved working at the company for the previous seven years and that I didn't want to leave. After all, I had worked incredibly hard to build a positive reputation and deliver results. However, at that time in my life, I needed more flexibility and no travel, so (deep breath) I assertively handed him my proposal (another deep breath) and said I would like to continue working with the group as a consultant.

As he read the one-page proposal for a project that I had created, I sat on the edge of my seat. The seconds slowly ticked by. I wished I could read his thoughts. *Would he question my loyalty and ask me to leave?*

Those next few seconds felt like an hour. Finally, he looked up.

"Lisa, we'd rather keep you than lose you," Sam said. "You know everyone on the team, so work with them and figure it out."

I exhaled.

And just like that, my consulting career had begun. I had a *lot* to learn.

You may be thinking, *Sure, consulting worked for you, but it couldn't possibly work for me.* You're unsure of what you would do or what it would look like. You aren't networked or experienced enough, or you don't live in a tech hub like Seattle. It feels foreign and risky. I get it. I've been there, too. I have helped thousands of people successfully shift to consulting, and every perceived obstacle that you're feeling is normal. I will show you how you can overcome your loudest doubts and realize success on your terms.

Expand your definition of work and get curious about what success really means to you—*right now.* Chances are, it's about much more than money and a title. With contract work, you can create your own definition of success. You can choose the work you love to do, and you have everything you need to make it happen. You can do this, and I will guide you every step of the way. A quote thought to be from Emily Dickinson sums it up: "One step at a time is all it takes to get you there."

Contracts and Consulting Defined

I chose consulting because it gave me the control I wanted over my work and life. Yet, when I first learned about consulting, it felt unattainable to me. I couldn't even wrap my head around what it was, exactly, let alone whether it was something I could do. You're likely feeling something similar. So, let's take a look at what consulting is and what it means to be a consultant.

The future of work has solidified the need for companies to access different types of talent from anywhere at any time. There are many consultancies, agencies, firms, and platforms of all sizes ranging from broad offerings to a specialized focus area that make up the world of external talent. Some offer employment and others work with subcontractors. Some provide zero support, others a white-glove experience. The growing universe continues to expand.

You will hear many terms used to describe external work, such as *project work*, *contract work*, and *gig work*. Each refers to discrete projects, or contracts, with a clear set of deliverables and desired outcomes.

Even more terms are used for the people who choose to work on contracts, including *consultants, freelancers, gig workers, independent workers, contractors, supertemps, fractional executives, on-demand experts, vendors,* and *temps*.

In this book, I'll refer to external work as *contracts* and *contract work* and the people who deliver this work as *consultants*.

Contract work has clear deliverables and desired outcomes that are outlined in a descriptive statement of work (SOW). Those deliverables may be paired with a time constraint—for example, a twelve-month contract to complete X, Y, and Z. They include things like a marketing plan or a website launch or a business strategy.

In my work at Simplicity Consulting, I advise clients to translate their goals into projects. This is a mindset shift from how we traditionally think of work. The roles that we're familiar with, including marketing director, web developer, and business strategist, comprise many tasks, or projects, with varying degrees of effort and ROI.

Think of projects as a spectrum ranging from small, one-off, or discrete tasks to big, ongoing, strategic work. Those small, well-defined projects with clear deliverables on the far-left end of the spectrum don't require much oversight, things like presentation or collateral design, photography, and minor website updates. On the other end of the spectrum are meaty, complex projects or those that support ongoing business needs. For example, a company may bring in a developer or even a small team of developers to create, test, and launch a new digital application.

Those projects are completed by outside experts we're calling *consultants*. Your initial mental image of a consultant may be similar to what mine was: A road warrior with an MBA and a high bill rate from a big, expensive consulting firm; someone with a shiny strategy deck who doesn't actually deliver the work. While that type of consultant and expensive, strategy-only consulting firm does exist, that's not what I'll focus on in the pages that follow.

This book centers on an increasingly growing breed of consultants who primarily have worked for corporations and choose to become a consultant. They're experts with enormous credibility who combine strategy (the vision) with execution (the work) to reach a goal. They excel at playing the role of strategic advisor, and they also love rolling up their sleeves and leveraging their skills, experience, and expertise to get the work done. They don't delegate, they do. I often refer to this type of consultant as a strategic doer.

Consulting is about delivering value every day. Consultants are hired for their expertise for a specific project with defined deliverables outlined in an SOW. They're evaluated by the outcome of those deliverables. Their work is typically strategic in nature and commands higher bill rates because clients need their proven expertise, though rates vary based on the supply and demand for an area of expertise. Consultants can work for themselves or with an intermediary, from small boutique agencies to global firms.

A consultant's primary goal? To make the client the hero. Consultants are extraordinarily focused on the client's needs and how they can make their client look great. They take a consultative approach to helping their clients identify gaps and solve problems. As a consultant, you're no longer in the spotlight. You're not the lead actor in this movie—you're playing the supporting role. Your success is directly proportional to your client's definition of success.

Viewing the client's success as your success requires a mindset shift. If you've worked in traditional corporate roles, you're familiar with navigating office politics and doing work that will be rewarded come review time. You're incentivized to climb the corporate ladder by titles, raises, and recognition. As an employee, saying *no* is rarely an option. The endless work and duties are expected, not requested.

It's worth understanding the general differences between the other common terms for on-demand experts. If you have the credibility to back it up, you can choose the term and title that match how you view yourself and your work. You are the CEO of your own career, and one of the advantages is choosing your title. We will discuss this in more detail, along with other personal branding considerations, in Chapter 3.

Contractors are typically placed by large staffing companies in staff augmentation roles. They tend to work on longer, more predictable projects that are role based and similar to the work done by employees they support. Companies typically hire contractors to maximize resource capacity.

Freelancers work for themselves as subcontractors. They choose this lifestyle for ultimate flexibility and can work directly with clients or through agencies on small or short-term projects. Freelancers have a specific area of expertise, such as design, writing, or software engineering.

Fractional executives are experienced professionals, often previous executives, hired on a part-time or short-term basis. They leverage their experience to cover a gap in an executive position or provide interim executive leadership until the company grows into needing a full-time resource in that role, most often seen at startups.

Depending on your background, experience and desired lifestyle, there are many options available to professionals today to choose how you want to work.

Do the Work You Love, on Your Terms

This is the book I wish someone had handed me when I first started out all those years ago. It would have saved me so much time and angst and built my confidence faster.

In the beginning, I learned by trial and error. I wrestled with negative self-talk. I asked questions, took opportunities, figured out my personal brand and built the plane while it was in flight. But you don't have to.

I wrote this book to teach you how to shortcut all that and give you the tools and knowledge to make it happen. You will benefit from my ten-plus years of experience and thousands of conversations, experiments, setbacks, wins, and learnings. This is not theory. These are proven principles and strategies that many talented professionals, like you, have leveraged to learn how to do the work they love, on their terms. Along the way, you will hear stories from actual consultants to inspire and motivate you in your journey.

This book is for any professional who is ready to own their career path. It is for the professional who wants to transition from full-time employment to consulting after years working in Corporate America. It's for the recent college graduate with specific skills looking to get a foot in the door and experience a range of different companies and cultures and for the millennials who enjoy the flexibility of contract work and the appeal of creating their own rules for work-life integration. It is also for the baby boomer with years of experience and wisdom who chooses to work due to financial necessity or a love of advising and mentoring others.

Trust your intuition. If there is a voice inside of you begging for a change, listen.

Life happens. If you're sick of missing family dinners or ballet recitals or soccer games, or done with chasing the next promotion, or exhausted from endlessly trying to force parenting and working into a finite amount of time, or fed up with the confines of the nine to five or the office politics or the administrivia . . . there is a different path.

Maybe you feel hopelessly stuck on the corporate treadmill, or you've lost your sense of purpose, but you don't see any other options. Or you followed your partner to a new town for his or her job, but you can't find anything locally that meets your needs. Or, after earning your degrees and thriving at work, you took time off to raise kids, and you're hitting a wall reentering the workforce. Maybe you're frazzled, burned out, and exhausted, and your confidence is at an all-time low. Or maybe you're slighted and angry because you got laid off, demoted, or passed up for that promotion you worked so hard for.

Whatever brought you to this book, I'm glad you're here. I want you to know that you have more options than ever before. Consulting *is* a viable alternative to traditional employment, and you already have everything you need to be successful. You have the opportunity to fit work into your life, instead of the other way around.

The best part? I'm your guide. *You* **are the star of this story. You already have everything you need to be successful.** I'll draw from my experiences to help you get there faster.

As with any strong building, we'll start with the foundation—the rock-solid base upon which everything is built. I'll help you define and share your personal brand, identify the work you love to do, your ideal project and client, and learn the art of the rate.

Once you've established that all-important foundation, then you take action. I like to think of it as a flywheel: those heavy, rotating mechanical wheels that power machinery with their momentum. Your actions—landing a contract, setting yourself up for success, delivering excellence, and reflecting and refreshing—will set your flywheel in motion. Your flywheel may spin slowly at first, and with each successful project and satisfied client, it gains momentum. As you grow and nurture your network and establish yourself as the go-to person in your area of expertise, your referral flywheel really starts spinning. I'll show you how to build that momentum to maintain a steady pipeline of contract work.

But first, let's assess if consulting is for you. I'll share the many considerations that factor into such an important decision. The following chapter outlines why people choose consulting, concluding with a brief assessment.

Let's get started.

TWO

IS CONSULTING FOR YOU?

"If you don't prioritize your life, someone else will."
—GREG MCKEOWN, *Essentialism*[1]

WHAT DOES SUCCESS LOOK LIKE for you *right now?* When I first transitioned to consulting, I wrestled with this question.

Up to that point, I'd focused on advancing my corporate career. I believed that earnings and titles were the definition of success. Yet, after fourteen years of achievement and two children, my definition of success began to shift. Climbing the corporate ladder became less important than intangibles like time, flexibility, and work with impact. I realized that flexibility and high-impact work were far more important to me at that point in my life and career than salary and a corporate title.

Many people experience similar shifts. Maybe your definition of success has shifted, too. We can't predict what life will throw at us. As much as we want to control our career and build a future-proof plan, life happens. Right now is all we have. Shift your focus from the future to your present and get in touch with what you want in this moment. In the next chapters, we'll discover the type of work that brings you the most joy and how you want to do that work.

I've always found joy in helping people. That constant has shown up in a variety of ways throughout my life across many different roles. Early in my career as a salesperson, I found joy in understanding my clients' needs and crafting solutions to their problems. As a consultant, I found joy in designing a life that allowed me to do work with impact while carving out time for my two young boys. Today, as a CEO, I find joy in helping others realize their greatness and giving them the support and opportunity to step into it. I also find joy in helping people, from graduates to career professionals, tap into and own their unique personal brands, so they can make their mark on the world.

In this chapter, we will explore the reasons people choose consulting and the common challenges they encounter. We'll also meet some successful consultants who have worked with me at Simplicity Consulting over the years. Each of their journeys is unique, and they've all made this alternative career path work for them. Throughout the book, they will share their successes and struggles to help you learn and grow. You may see yourself reflected in their stories, and I hope it gives you the added confidence to pursue the path that's right for you. We'll end with a short self-assessment to help you determine if consulting is right for you.

Why People Choose Consulting

Just as I did, many corporate professionals reach a place in their careers where they want to do the work they love on their terms. They're not interested in the administrivia and distractions of traditional full-time employment. They want more control. They intentionally shift to focus on doing great work and choose flexibility and purpose over golden handcuffs and the promise of career advancement.

Regardless of how people start consulting, intentionally or unintentionally, the benefits of the consulting lifestyle are near-universal. Let's explore several of them and meet some of our expert consultants. I'm so grateful to these professionals for sharing their wisdom with you.

Flexibility, Flexibility, Flexibility

Flexibility is the number one reason people love consulting. It's also the reason many choose it in the first place, whether by circumstance, such as parents of young kids or caregivers of sick or aging parents, or by choice—a desire to own their lives and control their time.

I've met with countless professionals over the years who loved their corporate careers but didn't love the inflexibility. They tried to carve out the flexibility they needed to stay, but their employer would not budge. They weren't willing or able to continue down a rigid path that didn't allow for the fluidity of life, so they left and found what they needed in consulting.

It's difficult to quantify just how valuable it is to choose how and when you want to work. You can choose to work part-time, full-time, every day, or a few days a week, half days or full days, moonlight on the side of your current full-time job, or any combination of those. Contract work is expansively flexible and dynamic, and you are in the driver's seat. You can control your earnings and make work adapt to your life by intentionally choosing the work you want to do. The flexible nature of consulting requires self-direction in often ambiguous environments. It is a good fit for people who work well independently and thrive on solving problems for a variety of clients and projects.

In contrast, working as a traditional employee generally doesn't offer much flexibility. It certainly varies by organization, but you're typically expected to be in meetings throughout the day and respond quickly to emails, calls, and Slack/Teams messages. It's ideal for professionals who value being part of a team, engaging with coworkers and managers, and climbing the corporate ladder, and it requires the ability to navigate corporate roadblocks and politics.

For many, flexibility isn't a nice-to-have, it's a need-to-have. For example, military spouses and so-called trailing partners can benefit greatly from flexibility. I've advised countless professionals who want to do impactful work and earn an income, but their career growth is constrained by frequent moves or living outside of an employment hub. One consultant I work with moved across the country when her husband was transferred to a different military base. Rather than being forced to quit her job and find something new in a completely different market, she was able to continue her work, virtually uninterrupted, from two thousand miles away. Now, that is flexibility! Despite being thrown into a new town with a baby, hours from a city with job opportunities, consulting allowed her to breathe a huge sigh of relief. And the continuity in one area of her life during a million other changes reaffirmed her commitment to doing great work.

I love the story of another consultant who decided to design her life around a roving RV. She travels the country with her husband while working on a contract with my company. She'll dial into meetings from Acadia National Park one week and the Grand Canyon the next. She is committed to showing up every day and delivering results to maintain the flexible lifestyle she craves.

Others take advantage of the flexibility to work from anywhere and move to places that feed their love for the outdoors or desire to live near family. Allison, a Montana native and marketing consultant, recognized this in her own lightbulb moment. One day, she realized that she didn't have to keep putting up with a nightmare commute, far away from her family—she could live anywhere. So, she quit. Allison traded her job for a consulting contract, and a few months later she moved back home to Montana. She's now been successfully consulting for more than a decade.

Another element of flexibility is the ability to take a "balloon approach" to work. Consulting enables you to control when to blow it up with multiple clients for variety or extra income to offset the risk, or deflate the work with a single part-time project due to life demands.

When I asked Keri, a marketing strategist for startups, how she consults with her family before "ballooning" her workload, she explained: "I sit them down and say, 'This big project came my way, and it's going to put me at capacity for the next six weeks. If I take it, here's what the next six weeks will look like and here's how I'll need you to step up. But it will also allow us to take that big trip we've been hoping for.'"

Layoffs or RIFs (Reductions in Force)

There are no guarantees in life or work. Many still believe that full-time employee roles are more secure than consulting contracts. However, layoffs have become commonplace. Mass layoff rates in the United States have climbed from 37.7 million in 1996 to 42.5 million in 2008. The COVID-19 pandemic is the most recent example. Roughly one in six US workers, or more than 26 million people, filed for unemployment during March and April 2020,[2] though McKinsey projects twice that number are "vulnerable"—a category that includes permanent layoffs, temporary furloughs, and cuts to hours and pay.

Just as we saw in the Great Recession of 2008, a subset of these newly unemployed professionals with marketable skills and expertise will turn to consulting or gig work. For some, it will be a short-term stopgap. Others will embrace the benefits of the consultant lifestyle and never look back.

It's important to note that we can't always predict which types of roles are the most vulnerable. For example, one of my clients made the difficult decision to lay off the entire product marketing team due to the coronavirus pandemic but didn't let go of a single one of the team's consultants. The immediate and business-critical work still needed to get done, so while they didn't have headcount for traditional employees, they did have the budget to continue the consultants' project work.

Deanna, a training and development expert, experienced this firsthand. Before she started working with me, a teammate's layoff helped her realize that she was more loyal to her employer than they were to her.

"We had a round of layoffs in our group, and I shared responsibilities with a woman who'd been on the team longer than me," she recalled in our video interview. "They let her go. It was the first time I'd been in a group where someone was laid off. I realized that I wanted more control. I thought, *If it's so easy for them to let her go, why am I holding on?*"

Deanna was tiring of her job for many reasons, but she stayed out of a sense of loyalty. Seeing her teammate let go—someone with a solid performance record and more tenure than her—was an eye-opener. She realized that her loyalty wasn't reciprocated by her employer. At the end of the day, as an employee at a global organization, she was ultimately a line on the budget.

As harsh as that sounds, it's the truth. I have seen too many professionals shocked by an unexpected layoff. They never saw it coming, no matter how good their work was.

Parenthood

Keri, our startup marketing strategist, quit her corporate job and started consulting after having her first child.

"I was probably a workaholic, and then throw a kid into the mix and there were just not enough hours in the day for the things I really cared about," she shared with me. "I realized I wasn't being the mom I wanted to be. And I just started seeing work differently. There was suddenly an opportunity cost: I could either make an impact somewhere or be with my kid. I knew I needed to somehow devise a plan where I could do both in what I felt was success for me. I felt very clearly that my purpose was not what I'd been doing. I needed something where I didn't have that opportunity cost. It was going to have to be something bigger and different."

I relate deeply to Keri's story because it's so similar to my own. It's not surprising, therefore, that consulting is an attractive option for professionals once they have kids, especially for working mothers.

Today, mothers bear the weight of several converging forces. They're working more: twenty-five hours a week on average, up from nine hours a week in 1965. But they're also spending more time on childcare—fourteen hours a week, compared to ten hours a week in 1965—in part because they feel increased pressure to be an involved parent (77 percent of women report this pressure, compared to 56 percent of men). And yet, more women are having children today than ten years ago: 86 percent of women give birth by age forty-four, compared to 80 percent a decade ago.[3]

Something's got to give.

Over the past decade and a half, Simplicity Consulting has employed 75 percent women on average, many of them mothers, seeking flexibility in their work. Some step away from the workforce for a few years to raise children, and consulting is a practical way to reenter the work world. Others, like Keri, continue working after having children, but scale back their hours or simply opt to work in a more flexible way to better juggle the demands of parenting and working.

Work, Not Politics

Kate is a writer. She quit her corporate gig to raise her two young children and write the book that had been swirling in her head during her daily commute. Now, as a consultant, she lights up when talking about her communications projects and geeks out on the ability to lose herself in the topic du jour.

"I just want to do the work," Kate told me. "I don't want to have to worry about all that other stuff."

That "other stuff" differs from company to company, but it includes things like performance reviews, office politics, administrivia, and endless meetings.

Every consultant I talked to for this book shared Kate's perspective. They all just want to focus on doing the work they love and doing it well. It's one of the reasons I chose consulting, too.

Side Hustle

Deanna loves how she's been able to create a schedule that allows space for her primary source of income, consulting, and her side hustle: career coaching.

"I have a lot of other interests I want to pursue outside of a full-time job," she said to me. "I have a career-coaching business for new and recent college graduates. I probably spend ten to fifteen hours a week doing that, and being able to get it going has been super exciting for me. Not feeling as beholden to a company and having some flexibility allows for other pieces of your life."

There's an entrepreneurial undercurrent to many consultants, myself included. In fact, nearly all the consultants I interviewed for this book have some form of side hustle, whether it is a hobby, passion, or a new business venture.

Allison is actively involved in local politics in her small Montana community, and she's shopping around for the right board to join. Kate wrote a young adult novel. Another invested in a commercial lighting company and yet another is paying the bills with her consulting contracts while getting her passion project—a blockchain banking solution for the unbanked—funded and fully off the ground. Another is feeding her creativity with a greeting card and jewelry business. All of them say that they would not have the time or mental energy to pursue their side hustles without the flexibility afforded by consulting.

This is what fuels me as an entrepreneur. I'm a creator at heart, and I love supporting people's big ambitions. It's inspiring to see people step into their dreams. I love helping those who intentionally choose to live life on their own terms and make a meaningful contribution to the world.

What if you could do the same while earning an income as a consultant?

Millennial Mindset

"Our generation has to be flexible because the world opened us up to the possibility that things can change at a moment's notice," said Hai when I asked him why millennials choose alternative career paths like consulting. "We have to plan for the future, but also plan for those plans to fall apart. Rather than scaring us from living to our fullest potential, those challenges made us realize that we need a plan B (and C) for everything."

Most everyone I talk to has a before story—the career they had or roles they did before getting into consulting—so I was fascinated to learn that Hai doesn't. A marketer at heart, Hai found a niche as a social and digital marketing expert with a passion for empathy. Consulting is the only way he's worked since graduating from business school.

Hai isn't alone. As you saw in the last chapter, a growing number of younger professionals are drawn to the consulting lifestyle. Unlike previous generations that expected to put in their time with a company and receive the obligatory watch when they retire, newer entrants to the workforce expect to work differently. They want flexibility in how they work, and they also want flexibility in their tenure with a company. Consulting feeds both those desires. Millennials have earned distinction as the "job-hopping generation." In a 2019 Gallup poll, 21 percent of millennials reported changing jobs within the past year—a rate three times higher than non-millennials.[4]

Hai has an interesting theory on why his generation is drawn to contract work.

"The collective challenges we've faced have shaped how we approach work," he said, citing monumental events like the advent of the internet, 9/11, the Great Recession, and the global economic impact of COVID-19.

My hunch is that, as more millennials and Gen Zs take root in the workforce, there will be fewer consultants with before stories. It will just be the way we work.

Choice

"I've really held out for the projects that I want," said Kate, the writer and executive communications consultant, on the fulfillment that's come with being able to choose her projects and shift her focus to social-good work. "And it's scary!" she added. "You feel like something comes your way, and you should take it, but waiting for the right one has been really rewarding."

As a consultant, you are in the driver's seat. You get to choose the work you want to do, who you want to do that work with, and how you do it. For Kate, that's allowed her to intentionally choose contracts that align with her values. She's worked on projects that highlight how tech is making an impact on accessibility efforts, climate change and carbon footprints, equality for the LGBTQIA+ community, and more. And, as long as she can continue to find work in this space, she plans to solely take social-good projects moving forward.

Conversely, as an employee you are often beholden to your manager and the leadership team and how they view your contributions to the organization. In that hierarchy with defined titles, paths, and structures, your manager controls your destiny and you have less choice of the type of work you do.

Variety

Keri loves how the variety of contract work feeds her inner builder.

"The thought of managing a holiday campaign for the fifth year in a row or a market launch for new-city-number-seventeen, it actually makes me feel physically a little sick," she told me with a grimace. "I like the new: launching the new brand, the new product, whatever it might be that makes a difference."

At Simplicity Consulting, we foster a growth mindset in our consultants and, as with Keri, it's a trait that's innate to many of them. Successful consultants are curious, lifelong learners. Perhaps that's why they value variety, whether in their clients, project type, project length, or all the above.

The nature of contract work allows you to explore different companies, industries, markets, and products. You can choose whether to stick with a specific niche or dabble in new and different areas. Contract work also enables you to gain new skills and get exposure to new and emerging technologies. This doesn't just benefit your personal growth. It also makes you more marketable for future contracts.

Focused Impact

Kate not only likes doing the work, she likes the opportunity to get into flow. When I talked with her for this book, she had spent the previous eight weeks wading through accessibility materials. And she was thrilled about it. Her client hired her to refresh the company's accessibility storytelling, an important project that her client didn't have bandwidth to take on.

"I was able to completely focus and own it end-to-end," she raved. That focus paid off. Within the first five minutes of her client's annual summit, the company's chief accessibility officer used Kate's content on stage. "Thousands of people saw that," Kate said. "It was great."

Like Kate, I remember realizing the power of focus after my first consulting project. I had handed off my deliverables, and my client was showering the work with praise. While I was proud of my work, I couldn't help thinking, *I was successful because I could focus. It was my whole job to do that one thing really well.*

Employees don't have that luxury. Employees are pulled in a million different directions responding to incessant emails and requests. They manage multiple workstreams and competing priorities. Endless meetings. Company trainings. Management responsibilities and annual reviews. As a consultant, you are freed up to focus on meaningful work with impact and only that, without those other distractions.

Common Challenges

While consulting has considerable benefits, I would be remiss if I didn't share some of the obstacles people face as consultants. As great as this path can be, it's not all butterflies and rainbows. Here are the top challenges that I consistently hear from consultants.

Instability and Change

"It still makes the planner in me crazy," shared Keri, the startup marketing strategist. "I set goals every year, but I can't predict how much money I'll make."

As a consultant, especially an independent one like Keri, it can be difficult to forecast when you will have work and how much you'll earn. A financial plan and reserve savings are important because you cannot control when projects will come your way. And, because you're only as good as your last project, you have to show up and add value each and every day. There's no kicking back and riding out an annual salary. You need to be on top of your game in every client interaction and in every project.

For many, the uncertainty doesn't go away—you just get better at planning for it.

"I've felt that uncertainty every single time a project is ending. No matter how great I do and that I'll have a good recommendation, it doesn't go away," admitted Kate. "I still think about the next project. We always take that uncertainty into account in our lifestyle because the project could end. But at the same time, there is no guarantee in any job."

As Kate notes, uncertainty isn't unique to contract work. The statistics and stories earlier in this chapter showed that the perception of stability in traditional employment is just that, perception. No job is 100 percent secure. Even if you do great work as an employee, management can always decide that your role is nonessential. Even then, severance isn't guaranteed. Despite what many think, you don't have full control over your career path as an employee.

Isolation

"The life of a consultant can be very isolating," said Allison in our video chat, her at home in Montana and me in my home office outside Seattle. "How much of a family do you need in your work world? I'm single, so my work people are really, really important to me."

Allison is right. Consulting can be lonely at times. Though some client teams are more welcoming and inclusive than others, it can feel as if you're on the outside looking in.

For me and the consultants I spoke with for this book, it's about trade-offs. What do you value more: Flexibility with your time and schedule, or a sense of belonging within a team and an organization? There's no right or wrong answer, but the trade-offs are real. Every consultant has his or her thing (or things!) for combatting the solitude.

Visit your client. It's often both refreshing and a reminder why you don't go into the office every day. Schedule lunch or happy hour with friends or your client team. Lean into hobbies and interests. Create or join a professional organization or meetup group. Work from coffee shops or coworking spaces. Take a class or learn a new skill. Volunteer. Mentor. Whatever it is, build the level of social interaction you need into your life.

Traditional Advancement and Development

Keri misses elements of her corporate career, especially receiving feedback and managing people.

"Really, the only feedback you get in consulting are the project extensions and referrals," she said. "Those are great, and they make you proud, but they're not the same. And I really miss managing people. I love to mentor and coach."

It's true: There's no performance review or regular feedback loop or annual bonus or salary raise in consulting. There's no clear career path with set titles or goals for managing people and leading teams.

There's no professional development program or budget either. It's up to you to determine what skills you want to develop and proactively seek out learning and development opportunities to up level your skills.

"You don't always feel like you're moving up; sometimes you're moving horizontally," Kate told me, when our conversation turned to career progression. "You just have to deal with that ambition in yourself and realize that you're moving up in other places."

Ambition doesn't go away when you become a consultant. But it expresses itself in different ways than chasing the next title or promotion.

Benefits

Twenty-two percent of freelancers cite affordable healthcare as their top concern with their way of working.[5] For those without a partner's benefits to lean on, healthcare and the other benefits of full-time employment can be a significant stressor.

However, being a consultant doesn't mean that you have to give up on employer-sponsored benefits. If you need benefits, look for a consultancy or agency that can offer you W-2 employment—they exist. Also, seek out the Affordable Care Act as another option.

I'm proud to offer benefits to the consultants who work with me at my company. Unless they opt to work as a 1099 subcontractor, the majority of our consultants are W-2 employees with all the benefits of full-time employment, including medical, dental, vision, life insurance, PTO (paid time off), and 401(k) matching. They get the best of both worlds: benefits and the flexibility to do the work they love.

Disrespect

It's not universal, but it's worth knowing that some employees may look down on you as a consultant. I've never really understood this, but it's happened to me, too. I have heard things like, "Isn't that consulting thing beneath you?" Whatever the reason for these snide comments or attitudes, it usually isn't about you, it's their own insecurities. Some are threatened by an expert they perceive as more capable than them. They may think you're vying for their job even when you're not. Or maybe they think consultants can't get a "real job."

Kate experienced this when she announced that she was leaving her job to devote more time to her young kids and to writing a book. Shortly after, a younger woman on the team approached her.

"She was disappointed in me!" Kate recalled. "She said, 'Oh, my gosh, I thought you were so hardcore. I can't believe you're leaving!' I think she thought I'd just be eating bonbons and working out a lot. I thought, *I'm writing a book and raising two young kids. What can be more ambitious than that?* But in taking a step out, I'd let her down in some way."

Kate took a break for a year and a half, spent time with her kids, and wrote her young adult book. She got back into the workforce as a consultant and found her niche. She's now living her own personal definition of success, one where she's happily balancing family, healthy eating and exercise, and continuous learning at work.

As a consultant, you don't have to work with people who treat you poorly. In fact, most of the consultants I spoke with for this book, Kate included, won't. Stay confident, know your worth, and keep your head up. There are so many wonderful and appreciative clients who are grateful to have experienced and committed consultants to help them realize success. Choose them, and your work life will be much happier.

And that woman who'd been disappointed to learn Kate was leaving her job?

"I ran into her a few years later," Kate said. "She had a two-year-old child, and she said, 'I want to talk to you about consulting.'"

Kate's role-model status had been reinstated.

Make It Count

We all have unique and valuable skills that the world needs. It's time for you to tap into yours. It is up to you to do the work outlined in this book and to understand and own what success means for you, right now. Not in the past, not ten years from now, but right now. Because all we really have is now.

This book will empower and equip you to build your confidence and credibility, define your personal brand, identify what success looks like for you, and help you successfully navigate the future of work to find contract work you love.

As Mary Oliver asked, "Tell me, what is it you plan to do / with your one wild and precious life?"[6]

This is your moment. Make it count.

Quiz: Is Consulting for Me?

So far, we've covered the *what* and *why* of consulting. Hopefully, your interest is piqued. Maybe you even saw yourself in one of the consultant stories. But you may still be unsure if consulting is right for you. Perhaps you're thinking, *Freedom and flexibility sound great, but is consulting right for me? How do I know?*

Take the quiz.

The following questions are grounded in my experience helping thousands of professionals determine whether consulting is the right fit for them. These questions can help you, too. I created the quiz based on the ABCs of what clients want in a consultant: Attitude, Build trust, and Communication. I developed the ABCs in 2010 after surveying clients to identify the core attributes they valued in great consultants. A decade later, these attributes have not changed. What made a great consultant then is what makes a great consultant today.

Ask yourself:

1. Am I a proactive self-starter?
2. Am I resilient?
3. Do I have an entrepreneurial mindset?
4. Do I have a positive, can-do, roll-with-the-punches kind of attitude?
5. Do I love exposure to different companies, cultures, people, and experiences?
6. Am I comfortable with change and uncertainty?
7. Am I financially and emotionally prepared for the ups and downs of contract work?
8. Do I have an area of expertise?
9. Do I love doing the work, rather than overseeing and managing it?
10. Do I have a strong network and a positive reputation?
11. Do I have a solid track record of accomplishments?
12. Am I a good listener?
13. Do I have a high EQ (emotional quotient)?
14. Am I comfortable adapting to others' work styles and expectations?
15. Am I comfortable in a supporting role where the client, not me, gets the glory and recognition?
16. Can I create a statement of work with clear deliverables?
17. Can I prioritize my workload and communicate consistently with my client or manager?
18. Am I comfortable setting boundaries and clear expectations?

19. Am I prepared and equipped for difficult and productive conversations with my client?

20. Can I convey my key points in writing? Or verbally?

If you answered *yes* to fifteen or more of these questions, congratulations! Consulting is likely a good path for you.

If you answered any of the questions *sometimes* or *no,* then sit with those questions. How did you feel when you read those questions? Are you open to learning how to address those areas? Over the course of this book, I will help you build these skills and, more important, build your confidence in your existing skills and experience. You can overcome any obstacle, and I will show you how. All you need is an open mind.

Let's Get Started

We covered a lot of ground in this chapter. Now the fun begins. I hope you are curious and eager to learn, because I'm excited to share with you everything I know about what it takes to be a successful consultant. This book will answer all your questions and more. I'll give you practical, actionable tools to make consulting work for you.

Next, we build your foundation, starting with defining your personal brand, then your ideal work, client, and rate. This phase is critical to invest in before jumping to the flywheel, so don't cheat yourself. Take your time. The foundation is yours alone to build. Once set, you will find it easier to thrive. Think of it like the foundation of a house—when stable and solid, the house will stand strong. If cracked, however, the house will not stand the test of time. Let's lay your solid, authentic foundation.

You can do this.

PART II
The Foundation

THREE

BUILD YOUR
PERSONAL BRAND

"Be yourself. Everyone else is already taken."
—ATTRIBUTED TO OSCAR WILDE

ATHARINE WAS AT A CROSSROADS. She had risen through the ranks at a global public relations agency before stepping out onto the mommy track. Now, after a ten-year break in full-time employment—doing freelance communications projects here and there—her kids were entering junior high, and she was in the midst of a divorce. She wasn't sure where and how to step back into the work world.

She kept coming back to the three burning questions that had been swirling around in her head: *What am I good at? What do I love? What does the world need?*

As she asked herself those questions, she remembered the thing she had taught her kids: Don't try to be great at everything. Focus on what you're great at and forget the rest.

Since she knew the agency world, it was the first door she opened. She'd waited to have kids so she could focus on her career, and she'd been a vice president when she left. She enjoyed the work, and she'd been good at it, too.

I'll go back to agency life, she thought, *and find a senior leadership role and pick up where I left off.*

However, when she reached out to an executive from her old agency, he gave her the advice she didn't know she needed.

"You'll be sitting in a conference room all day reading spreadsheets and determining how billable everybody is," he cautioned. "I know you, and you would hate that."

Catharine will never forget that conversation. He knew her and her working style well. And he was right!

"There's not an administrative or managerial bone in my body," she told me with a laugh. "I'm not someone who'd be super jazzed about managing a team of twenty people. That's my worst nightmare."

"Don't do something just because you think you should," he advised her. "Find what you're great at and go do it."

So, at this crossroads in her adult life, she began to refocus on the thing she'd always been great at—writing.

Even in elementary school, people told Catharine that she was a great writer. It was easy for her. Her great-grandmother had been a writer. Catharine's mother had traveled to Chicago and then England to earn a master's degree in English, which was pretty radical for a girl from Iowa in the early sixties, Catharine notes. Throughout her career, writing was what she became known for.

Catharine leaned into her love of writing. It was the thing that lit her up. She had always loved doing the work, from setting the strategy to getting lost in the creative. In journalism school, Catharine had been drawn to storytelling, and as she began consulting, she started to get the sense that storytelling could be a gamechanger for brands and organizations.

"I didn't invent the term," she was quick to tell me. "But I could sense that storytelling was about to explode onto the scene. When your ear is tuned to hear something, you're going to hear it faster."

Today, Catharine is a successful consultant at Simplicity. When anyone on our team thinks about Catharine, they think first about her storytelling. She's incredible at it. It's her personal brand. It's who she is, how she positions herself, and the thing she loves to do.

"I learned to appreciate the artist at the core of who I am," she said.

For Catharine, knowing your personal brand is about knowing and trusting yourself. Her ability to recognize and refine her brand has enabled her to create impact for her clients.

Catharine helps companies and leaders define and tell their unique stories. Her storytelling has empowered C-suite executives and global luminaries to discover, strategize, create, and deliver their most powerful narratives to drive business results and spark action. It has advanced voices of freedom with the Oslo Freedom Forum. It has crafted speeches for the Grace Hopper Celebration of Women in Computing. It has guided speakers and informed messaging for huge global events. From individual brands to the Fortune 500, it has helped people shine so they can change the world.

Each of us is unique and multifaceted, so choose your personal brand wisely. It needs to feel exciting and authentic to you. Every person has unique gifts and talents to offer the world. It's why I wrote the *Personal Brand Playbook*: to help people discover and own their brand in order to reach their personal definition of success.[1] It was developed from thousands of conversations with experienced professionals who had rarely previously thought about what they stood for. The idea of a personal brand was foreign to them. Most of the time when I ask people about their personal brand, they have a hard time describing it, but it's always in plain sight.

"You have a lot of great experience," I'd say. "Of all the work you've done, what work lights you up? What work do you want to do right now?"

I am typically met with blank stares. Most people are dumbfounded. They have never been asked that before and couldn't I please just tell them what to do?

No, I can't. That's the beauty of being a consultant—*you* get to choose. To stand out and attract clients, you must first decide what you stand for. And then articulate that clearly, consistently, and proudly.

That's what we're going to do in this chapter, and that's why I developed this framework. I'll guide you through the five simple steps to define your personal brand. I know what you're thinking: *Personal brand? That sounds hard and overwhelming. I'd need the full muscle of a marketing agency to come up with a good personal brand. Do I really have to do this?*

Trust me, it's not as hard as you may think, and you already have everything you need to make it happen.

Take a deep breath. You can do this. Your personal brand is an authentic reflection of you, so take the pressure off yourself because there are no right or wrong answers. It requires taking a moment to pause and reflect. It is internal work that can't be rushed and evolves over your lifetime. It demands vulnerability. As Brené Brown, the queen of vulnerability research, said, "Vulnerability is our most accurate measurement of courage."[2] It's courageous to choose what you want to be known for. And once you do it you will feel limitless. Your personal brand is the intersection of your strengths and your passions.

Your personal brand is your strength plus your passion.

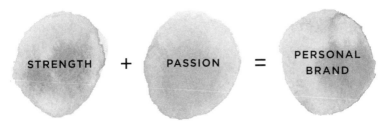

It's about what you're really good at and what you love to do. I've advised many professionals with years of successful work experience who struggle with the idea of personal brand. What they don't realize is that they've already been building it along the way, intentionally or not. Personal brand is the combination of the work you do, your reputation, and the things that energize you. That is why choosing jobs you love where you can demonstrate success is so important, because you are building your brand every day.

What We Can Learn from Great Brands

As Seth Godin puts it, "If you want to stand for something, you can't stand for everything."[3]

One of the most important lessons we can learn from successful brands is that it's not only okay to not be everything to everyone, it's critical to your success to put a stake in the ground and stand for something.

Sometimes that means narrowing your brand until it feels uncomfortable. We all like to have options, but as Catharine intuited at the start of the chapter, this strategy of being everything to everyone means you appear too generic in the marketplace. Go too broad, and you don't stand out.

Before we get into building your personal brand, we are going to learn from great brands in the marketplace that stand out. Think about brands you're attracted to. What makes them stand out? What attributes do you value in those brands? When I teach my personal brand workshop, there are a few common brands that people recall.

Great Brands Tell a Clear, Consistent Story

One brand that people consistently share is Nordstrom. And when I ask what it is about Nordstrom, they say customer service. It's a strength that the company has intentionally decided to be known for. It's not something they just talk about, it's something they do. Nordstrom has integrated superior service into every aspect of the customer experience. It's in their return policy, curbside pickup, in-store service, personal shopping, and more. All these things ladder up to an exceptional retail experience that puts the customer first.

Now, not everyone cares about customer service and those who don't may not feel attracted to Nordstrom. But, by putting a stake in the ground and standing for it every time, Nordstrom is standing out. It is clearly and consistently differentiating its brand and attracting customers who *do* value a high level of service. The company is also making the conscious choice to deprioritize customers who don't.

Great Brands Stand for Something

Nike is consistently ranked as one of the world's most recognizable brands. We all know that iconic swoosh and the "Just do it" tagline.

Their mission is to bring inspiration and innovation to every athlete in the world. They are all about empowerment, and they take it seriously.

Here's a good example: When Nike intentionally decided to stand for racial justice. Remember its controversial ad campaign in 2018?

> *Believe in something, even if it means sacrificing everything.*
> —COLIN KAEPERNICK

The campaign was viewed by many as too risky for a well-established brand. Social media blew up with reactions. People either loved it or hated it. And sure, Nike did lose some fans who posted angry videos online of themselves burning Air Jordans in protest.

But Nike gained more than it lost. A lot more. The company reported $163 million in earned media, a boost in brand value of $6 billion, and a 31 percent increase in sales.[4] The ad even won an Emmy.[5] Those customers who believed in protesting racial injustice felt a stronger loyalty to Nike for taking such a bold stand, and Nike was perfectly fine with those customers who did not support their point of view.

Great Brands Live Their Values

Patagonia is grounded in the core values of sustainability and caring for the environment. The company is more than just clothes and climbing gear, it's a movement.

In fact, Patagonia puts its values before its bottom line. The brand's foundational value? *We are in business to save our home planet.* For Patagonia, that plays out in many ways, all of which are radical for a clothing-and-gear company.

It's built a Worn Wear program that instructs you to drop old gear "in the mail, not the landfill" for store credit. Patagonia's own website encourages you to "buy only what you need, buy local when possible and repair what you already own." The company once took out a full-page ad in the *New York Times* on Black Friday declaring "DON'T BUY THIS JACKET" to address consumerism and discourage needless consumption.[6] It believes so strongly in fighting climate change that all its New York City stores closed for most of the day on September 21, 2020, so employees could participate in the People's Climate March.[7]

Nordstrom, Nike, and Patagonia are very different brands, each with a clear differentiation and target customer. They go to market with a clear value proposition and make no apologies about who they are and what they stand for. By doing this, they attract like-minded customers who feel connected and loyal to their brand. They are not trying to be everything to everyone but instead be the best at what they have set out to focus on.

What can we as people learn from great brands? We can learn that being true to our authentic selves is our power. And it's up to each of us to identify it and own it.

What do *you* stand for?

I'll ask guiding questions to help you answer that. All of it comes down to this: Embrace your greatness. Be the best at whatever it is that you love and likely feels easy. It's often something that may be effortless for you and you've been doing for years. Just like Catharine, who always knew she was a great writer, but it took time to finally recognize and step into it as her superpower. It's common to overlook the strengths that come naturally to us and focus instead on developing skills that are harder for us to master.

Don't get me wrong: I am a big fan of personal and professional development and lifelong learning, but don't overlook what comes easily to you because it's often your greatness. And the world needs your greatness. Let's get into it so you can articulate your unique personal brand with confidence and credibility.

Root Work

I like the analogy of a tree for personal brand work.

Think about your personal brand as a root structure—the internal, below-the-surface work that's only seen by you; the all-important foundation without which the tree literally cannot stand.

One of the biggest mistakes I see consultants make is not taking the time to do this foundational root work. It's a mistake that often leads them down a dark and lonely path. Before pursuing the work you want, you must understand your personal brand and believe in your greatness. If you don't believe in yourself, nobody else will.

Did you know that it can take as long as eighteen months for roots to develop underground before a tree appears on the surface? Your root work won't take nearly that long, but you will need to build your solid foundation before your tree can flourish above ground for all to see. Be patient with yourself and the process.

The above-the-ground work is covered in Part III of this book— the Flywheel section. And while it's tempting to skip the rest of this tree analogy and go straight there, don't.

Great consultants have one thing in common: a clearly defined personal brand that gives them the confidence and credibility to attract the work they want. That foundational work of building a brand must come first. Without it, the magic of landing the work and life you want may be elusive.

So, settle in. Get comfortable. Take the time to get to know yourself. Have fun reflecting on what makes you tick. You will be a better and more marketable consultant because of it. I'm excited for you to unearth and own your greatness.

Be You: Five Steps to Building Your Personal Brand

The five steps crystallized in my tiny rented office. It was my first real workspace after leaving my corporate job, and it gave me the silence to focus away from all the distractions that come with two little boys at home. I'd been teaching my weekly Consulting 101 class for more than a year, and by then I had observed common questions people were asking. I also noticed that most people were trying to be everything to everyone, which wasn't helping them stand out and land contracts. I kept thinking that I needed to help them articulate their unique strengths and motivations, their personal brand, before they started trying to find contract work. The result is the five steps, and they haven't changed for more than ten years. These are evergreen questions that I invite people to return to often as an opportunity to check in with themselves and make sure they are in alignment with the work they truly want to do.

As I said in Chapter 1, I wish someone had given me this book when I was first starting out in consulting. Personal brand is a big reason for that. I wish I'd known from the start how to articulate my personal brand and land work that aligned with it. I wish I'd had the tools to more quickly boost my confidence and own my greatness.

But now you have this book and the tools for building a rock-solid personal brand.

"Don't worry about what the world needs, ask what makes you come alive, and go do it, because what the world needs are people who have come alive," said Howard Thurman,[8] legendary American author, educator, and civil rights leader. I love this quote because we are so bombarded with shoulds and keeping pace with others that we rarely slow down to ask, What do I want? What really lights me up? What brings me joy at work?

And guess what happens when you find that thing you love to do that feels so effortless? It energizes you, and that energy will attract people who need those skills. Your passion and purpose will speak volumes, making it clear that you're intentionally choosing this work, rather than forcing yourself to do something that doesn't spark joy.

Those intentional choices are at the heart of your personal brand. I still remember the thrill I felt when I started consulting and got to choose with whom to work. What a joy! The ability to select the people and the projects that you want to work on is a gift. And so is the ability to say no to the things that you don't like. You can't say no when you're a full-time employee. That's not to say that you won't work with some difficult people as a consultant, but you can choose where to focus your time and energy on clients and work that lights you up.

I'll guide you through the five steps to build your personal brand: Be aware, be unique, be confident, be teachable, and be kind. Take a moment to pause and reflect with each step. I invite you to take notes, write down whatever is meaningful to you in the moment, and revisit these questions as often as you need, because your personal brand is always evolving.

Step One: Be Aware

The first step is building awareness of how you show up and recognizing how your actions are aligned with your intentions. We all see the world through rose-colored glasses based on our life experiences, and our unconscious decision making profoundly impacts how we show up every day.

As a reminder, I define personal brand as the intersection of your strengths and passions. Nailing that combination hinges on recognizing how you show up and how people perceive you, and then making sure that the brand you're projecting aligns with how you want to be seen.

We've all had friends or coworkers who think their brand is one thing, but their actions tell a very different story. It's disorienting. When your brand and actions aren't in alignment, it shows. You want to be sure that your brand narrative and the work you're doing tell the same story, because when we're consistent, the right people find us, and they know exactly what they're going to get.

QUESTION: Who do I admire and why?

Think of someone you admire. This person could be someone you work with or someone you've observed from afar, past or present. The key is to identify the qualities this person possesses that attract you to them.

We can learn a lot about what's important to us by identifying our role models. For example, I admire Oprah Winfrey. She's genuine and a powerful leader, and she's devoted her life to helping others. She's built a successful career on her own terms, and she's embraced her authentic self. Those attributes are important to me and serve as a North Star to guide my actions.

QUESTION: What are my authentic words?

Next, take that list of aspirational qualities, clues about what you want reflected in your personal brand, and think about which of those words you want to be known for. Are there any other words that resonate when you think about your authentic words? Write them down and circle the top three.

Being aware of these authentic words will help you distill your personal brand story. In a bit, we'll get into where and how to tell that story consistently. As you think about building your brand and what you stand for, use those attributes as building blocks. And if any of those words really resonate with you, circle them. If there are other words that come to mind, write them down. Those are your authentic words.

But for now: These are the words to highlight on your LinkedIn profile. They are the words to say when you talk with a potential client or introduce yourself in an interview.

If you can, narrow them down to three words. Then, when someone asks you to describe yourself, you can say, "I'm authentic, creative, and resourceful, and here's why." They're likely going to remember those three words and share them with others.

It sounds obvious, but we must be clear about who we are and how we want to be seen. Make it easy for people—give them the words rather than just hope they'll come up with those words on their own.

And those words have power! Whether you wrote down *authentic* or *genuine* or *creative* or *fun*, the words that you use to describe yourself will soon become the words that others say about you, too.

For women, especially, this is huge. I've worked with so many women over the years who are quick to dismiss compliments, and I'm one of them. We say things like, "Oh, it wasn't a big deal. Everybody can do this. I'm not that good at it." We rarely allow ourselves to truly acknowledge compliments and recognize the things we are good at. Many women struggle with worrying about bragging about themselves when they are simply owning their accomplishments. Let's shift that. There's power in recognizing your gifts and in intentionally pursuing work that allows you to use those natural gifts. You can step into your greatness and do it in a confident, not arrogant, way. And it starts with naming and celebrating your authentic words.

Step Two: Be Unique

You have greatness within you, and it's likely that you overlook it. I'm excited for you to rediscover your strengths.

For Catharine, that strength is writing and storytelling. It took me a while to recognize my strength around building partnerships. After all, I had done it my whole life, but it was only when I became a consultant that I realized it was a unique strength. In my corporate jobs, I was given the difficult clients to turn around and realized that was a differentiator. Not everyone can turn around bad relationships, but I loved doing it and I was really good at it.

What's yours? What is so easy for you to do that it's almost effortless? What skill or expertise do people routinely turn to you for?

Maybe it's spreadsheets. Or building websites. Or closing deals. Or making order out of chaos. Or managing budgets.

Whatever it is that you're good at, own it. Everyone has natural strengths, and if you are struggling with recognizing yours, then I encourage you to ask people who know you and whom you trust, ideally work colleagues, what you are really good at. They will tell you. Also, you may find clues in your previous annual reviews. Usually you will find consistent feedback about your strengths over the years from managers.

Just make sure it's both a strength and a passion. I've had people tell me that they're really good at spreadsheets but that they don't want to do that kind of work anymore. In that case, stop telling people you're good at spreadsheets! Identify another skill you love that's effortless and tell that story instead.

QUESTION: What am I the go-to person for?

What is effortless for you? What have people always told you that you're great at?

Step Three: Be Confident

As First Lady Eleanor Roosevelt is credited with saying, "Nobody can make you feel inferior without your consent." When I first started consulting, I struggled with gremlins and self-doubt. *Who was I to be a consultant? What did I know about consulting? What if I failed?*

And I wasn't the only one questioning myself. I remember bumping into an executive, a man I'd sat across from for years, in the office lobby one day, a few months after I returned from maternity leave . . . as a consultant.

"Why would you ever leave?" he asked. "Why did you choose to take a step down?"

He thought I'd lost my mind. But I smiled, because I knew this was what I wanted even if he didn't understand my motivations.

"I love being a consultant," I said with a smile. "Want to hire me? I'll make you look great!"

Confidence is conviction in yourself about your choices. It's okay if others don't understand your decisions—you don't have to explain anything to anyone. It's your life, so listen to yourself and be confident in your choices.

You will have all kinds of people throwing judgments and "shoulds" at you about your life. I've learned that people's opinions usually have nothing to do with me—it's about them and how they see their life. When people would say things to me such as, "How could you quit a good job for the unpredictable world of consulting?" I realized that comment was about their own fear of insecurity, not mine. Once I let go of other people's opinions of me and started listening to what I truly wanted, it helped build my confidence. I knew I had made the right decision for me, my family, and my career. Each successful project, each meaningful moment with my boys, and each person I helped along a similar path boosted my confidence.

Confidence breeds success and attracts others, including potential clients. I don't buy into the fake-it-til-you-make-it mentality. It feels inauthentic to me. I've found that the best way to channel confidence is to remember my success stories.

Your success stories are evidence of your greatness and your accomplishments. They bolster your confidence in interviews and client conversations. I recommend revisiting your stories when you've hit a roadblock or before an interview or important client meeting. Those stories are a surefire way to remind yourself of your greatness and boost your confidence.

You already have your top three authentic words. Next, define three success stories that correspond to each word. You can answer any question that a prospective client might throw at you by sharing your stories. What any client really wants to understand is who you are and if you have the skills and experience to solve their problem. They want to quickly and easily evaluate whether you have what it takes to deliver and if you can help them. You can effectively bridge their understanding by telling them true success stories of work you've done in similar or relevant situations.

When sharing your success stories you can say that you are known for creativity and then briefly describe a story of how your creativity solved a problem by explaining the challenge and the results. Or you can share that it sounds like the work you did with Company Z and how you approached that situation.

QUESTION:

What is your most memorable, professional, success story?

I'm sure you have many stories—think back to three different professional experiences that really stand out, when you felt on top of the world. Where were you? What were you doing? What were your contributions? How did you feel? What specific elements gave you the most happiness or pride?

Only highlight the stories that reflect the work you want to do more of right now. Take a moment to write down those stories, pairing those memories with specific metrics and outcomes.

How does it feel to recall those proud moments? I'm guessing it feels pretty good. It may have been a while since you've thought about your greatness, but it's still there, just waiting for you to own it.

Step Four: Be Teachable

As a consultant, it's up to you to proactively invest in yourself. Unlike in a corporate role, there's no training department or professional development stipend. Nobody is reminding you to go invest in yourself. Your passions and curiosities dictate what and when you learn. Great consultants commit to lifelong learning and make it a habit.

Being teachable is about identifying in which areas you want to build your skills and where you want to learn and grow right now. Maybe you want to advance your mastery of a subject in which you're currently working. Maybe you're excited to develop skills in an area that's new to you.

There are many ways to learn and grow, so decide what works best for you. It could require attending a conference, so budget for the registration fee and put the dates on the calendar. If it's a course, push yourself outside your comfort zone and sign up. If it's a book or podcast, build in time to consume, digest, and act on the content. Whatever it is, be intentional about the skills you choose to grow, and set aside the time and mind space to nurture them. Always be curious. This allows you to bring new insights to your clients and keeps you motivated.

I love podcasts, so I intentionally seek out shows and episodes that build my knowledge base while I'm walking my dog, Winston, or folding laundry. I know that when I invest thirty minutes of my time with Guy Raz on *How I Built This* or Michael Barbaro on *The Daily*, I'll learn something new.

Mentors are a great way to learn from someone that you admire. Throughout my career, I've been both a mentor and a mentee, and I always learn something from others. While both sides of the equation require some time and energy, the mentor–mentee relationship has always helped me to grow and see a new perspective. If you don't ask, the answer is always *no*, so take the initiative to reach out to those people whom you admire and feel you can learn something from.

Tips for reaching out to a prospective mentor:

Be specific. Be clear about what you're asking for. For example, "I admire how you've grown your company's organic press coverage. I'd like to buy you coffee once a quarter to ask how to successfully pitch media outlets."

Do your homework. Don't ask questions that a simple Google search can answer. Brush up on the topic, so you can ask informed questions. It's even better if you can send your questions ahead of time so the mentor can think about a response and be more efficient.

Respect their time. Schedule a short time window, thirty minutes or less, and stick to it. Arrive on time, listen, and take notes. Don't forget to follow up with a thank-you email, describing briefly what you learned.

There are many ways to invest in yourself. Here are some ideas. Choose what works for you.

- Podcasts
- Trade publications
- Conferences
- Workshops
- Courses (self-guided or facilitated)
- LinkedIn Learning (online courses)
- Internships
- Mentorship
- Books
- Video tutorials
- Shadowing an expert
- Meetup groups
- Industry/professional organization events, trainings, and content

If you're not sure where to start, reach out to a peer you admire. Ask for recommendations on what to read, listen to, watch, or engage with to grow your skills.

QUESTION:

What is one thing I will do today to build my skills?

Step Five: Be Kind

The final step is all about being kind to yourself. We have just spent time developing your beautiful personal brand—being kind is about you believing it and owning it, because if you don't believe it, no one will.

I'm still learning how to practice self-care. When I make the effort to carve out time for myself, I notice it makes a big difference in supporting how I want to show up every day. That self-awareness is critical. My mind tends to race and spin with ideas, and I can overwhelm and exhaust myself. Now when I recognize this feeling, I pause and spend a few minutes using a meditation app. Guided meditation helps calm my mind, focus on my breath, and restore my energy. Taking the time to quiet all that frenetic craziness has been a gamechanger for me. What works for you? Think about areas in your life where you may not be so kind to yourself and how you can take a small action to improve it.

Tame the Gremlins

We all have those not-so-helpful voices in our heads called many names, including *saboteur, gremlin, monkey mind, negative self-talk,* and *vocal inner critics*. Most of us may not notice these unconscious thoughts that have been running through our brains and bodies for years. At one point, those thoughts were there to protect you, but now they may be holding you back from who you really want to be, preventing you from owning your personal brand. You know what I'm talking about, right? Those thoughts that limit us from fully stepping into our brand. Here's my point: You don't have to believe everything you think. Isn't that empowering?

You've just identified powerful words and stories about who you are and how you want to be seen and contribute to the world, but none of that will work without self-compassion. Be kind to yourself and recognize those inevitable thoughts, such as, *Who am I to do that? Isn't consulting risky? What if I don't get any projects?* Or the catchall, *What if I fail?* Remember, these thoughts are normal; most everyone has self-limiting thoughts. Get used to watching them like white, fluffy clouds floating across the blue sky, but do not become them.

Focus on What You Can Control

Many things in this world are within our control. Stress and the gremlins creep in when we try to manage those things that are outside our control, things like if that client will hire you or when someone will call you back or when a contract will start. Let those things go. Instead, focus on what you can influence, such as how you talk about yourself and the actions you take every day to support your personal brand.

I've observed consultants who get stuck in a negative self-talk cycle when a client doesn't call back or they are frustrated by the snail's pace of a budget approval. I get it. But it's not about you. While self-awareness is important, usually there are many factors out of your control that have nothing to do with you. It's not personal, although it can feel that way.

We don't like feeling uncomfortable and uncertain, but you always have a choice. You can choose to live either in fear or opportunity. I encourage you to be aware of your thoughts and where you're focusing your energy, because that empowers you to use your time most effectively and efficiently. After all, your time is a nonrenewable resource.

QUESTION: What is the one thing
I will do for myself every day to restore my energy?

Think about the one thing that you're going to do for yourself on a regular basis to recharge and increase your energy. Write it on a sticky note, put it in your calendar, or do whatever you need to prioritize you.

Personal Brand Statement

Let's close by putting it all together with your personal brand statement.

> I am a <what> who <why>.

Your *what* is the thing you do. Your title, role, or work. Often, it's how you already introduce yourself. What people really want to know is your *why*. What's your motivation? Why do you do this work? What makes it meaningful to you?

Once you are clear on those two elements, you can interchange them and state them with confidence. The most important part of a powerful and unforgettable personal brand statement is that the words feel authentic to you. They must resonate with your soul. You know that feeling in the middle of your chest when you say a word that you feel deeply connected to? That's what you want to experience when you share your why.

Spend some time peeling back the onion. Many people start with a very long and formal-sounding statement. Keep going and ask yourself, *What really motivates me about that?* A great personal brand statement must emotionally resonate with you. If it doesn't, then it will feel hollow and inauthentic. You want to feel as if you are sharing a little bit of your soul.

Over time, your *what* will change as we have many different titles and roles throughout our working life, but your *why* is constant. There are many roles we can play to satisfy our *why*. You get to choose the role you want to play right now. Focus on getting your *why* right, and the *what* will take care of itself.

For example, in my nearly thirty-year career, I've discovered a common thread through my many titles and roles. Helping people—that's my why. I'm not sure I could have identified it when I was starting out, but it's clear now. When I reflect on my sales, account management, entrepreneurial and consulting roles, my motivation and purpose have always been to help people find success, and I've achieved this in different roles. My personal brand statement is grounded in that common thread: I am a founder, CEO, author, and speaker who is driven by helping everyone thrive in the new world of work.

Now it's your turn.

What is your current title? What is your motivation?

Here are some examples of personal brand statements for inspiration that I have heard many consultants share, starting with Catharine, whom you met at the top of the chapter:

I am a Storyteller whose dream is to help C-suite executives and global luminaries reach their dreams of influencing the world.

I am a Project Manager who loves creating order out of chaos.

I am a Business Analyst who thrives on helping leaders make sound decisions.

I am a Business Strategist who likes making a big impact by creating and developing a vision.

I am a CEO who loves helping people thrive at work.

I am a Sales Leader who enjoys people and building relationships.

I am a Content Marketer who helps brands I believe in tell their stories and grow their audiences.

You just completed the hardest part of the book. Building your personal brand can feel overwhelming, and you did it! That wasn't so bad, was it? Did you remind yourself about what motivates you and have fun remembering your success stories? These are your facts and evidence to own and be proud of. This is you! It may take some time and practice with your authentic words, success stories, and personal brand statement for you to believe your own greatness, but it's all there.

Author and activist Marianne Williamson spells out the power of owning your personal brand:

Our deepest fear is not that we are inadequate. Our deepest fear is that we are powerful beyond measure. It is our light, not our darkness, that most frightens us. We ask ourselves: Who am I to be brilliant, gorgeous, talented, fabulous? Actually, who are you *not* to be?[9]

Now that you have strengthened your confidence and credibility with a clear personal brand, you are ready to start crafting your ideal contract. You already have everything you need to do the work you love, so let's get to it.

Reflection Questions

- What are your authentic words?
- What is your personal brand statement?
- What are your professional success stories?

FOUR

DEFINE THE WORK
THAT FITS YOUR LIFE

"The only way to do great work is to love what you do.
If you haven't found it yet, keep looking."
—STEVE JOBS[1]

NOW THAT YOU'VE BUILT YOUR personal brand, let's take a holistic look at the factors that contribute to your ideal contract. Throughout this chapter, you will define how to fit work into your life, and not the other way around. I'll help you see how you can do the work you love, however you love to do it.

Let's say hello again to Allison, the Montana native and marketing consultant, whose lightbulb moment freed her to successfully fit work into her life. When I interviewed her for this book, she told me: "I love my life. My work doesn't define me, but it's one of those huge building blocks in the joyful life that I get to live."

It wasn't always that way. Long before she started working with me at Simplicity, Allison left her home in Montana and landed in Spokane for law school. As a law clerk while working toward her degree, she quickly realized that she was more interested in business than law.

A lot of it had to do with integrity. After law school, for example, she moved to Washington, D.C., where she worked for multiple law firms.

"One firm would fly me from D.C. to Los Angeles each week," she recalled, shaking her head. "And they would bill me to three different clients while I was in flight."

She left law, got her MBA in New York while working for a legal publisher, and later moved to Seattle after being recruited by a large tech company. Allison stayed there for a decade. She made good money, but life was stressful, her commute was bonkers, and her team environment at work was increasingly political and divisive. Plus, Seattle had gotten crowded, and she was now vying for solitude on her favorite trails.

And then she had her lightbulb moment.

One day while working at her living room table, she suddenly stopped typing and looked up. *Why am I still living here?* she asked herself. *I could live anywhere! I could live on a sailboat in Australia if I wanted, as long as I called into my meetings at the same time as my co-workers.*

So, Allison quit, took a consulting contract, and moved back home to Montana. She wanted work to fit into the life she desired, and she was determined to make it happen.

Though she was on her way to living the life she now loves, her consulting career got off to a bumpy start. The first agency she'd landed with encouraged consultants to get multiple full-time contracts, without the clients' knowledge. Not only was it exhausting to

Allison, it reminded her why she'd previously left law. That approach didn't align with her values. A friend referred her to Simplicity Consulting where she found values aligned with transparency, partnership, and autonomy.

Success to Allison is living in Big Sky Country, near her friends and family, doing work she loves for clients and an agency that share her same values.

"None of this would be worth any of it, if I didn't know I was doing great work that I'm proud of," she said. "It's aligned with my skill set in such a way that it brings joy. Do what you're good at. It doesn't have to be hard."

We often fall into the trap of thinking that our work must be difficult for it to be meaningful. And while Allison has worked incredibly hard during her career and has had periods with steep learning curves, she has embraced what is effortless for her: marketing communications.

We are also often content to work and live on someone else's terms. We're so consumed with the way it's always been that we forget we can define our ideal work life. Allison's story reminds me to be courageous and pursue the things that matter to me. You have the power to prioritize what matters most to you and define your ideal work life.

Be True to Your Brand

I admire Allison's clarity. It was a journey for her to achieve it, but she knows the work she loves to do and how she wants to do it. As you evaluate the work you love to do, trust your intuition. Be thoughtful about your brand, both how you want to be seen and what you want to do. Because going outside your brand and your core expertise can have consequences.

Early on in my consulting career, I took a six-month project outside my wheelhouse as a favor to a friend. They needed some operational help in a technical team, and although the project wasn't aligned with my brand, I figured it couldn't hurt to expand my horizons and build some new skills.

Once I got into it, I realized I was out of my league. I hadn't scoped the work properly, and I spent many late nights teaching myself as I went. The work was far more technical than I anticipated, and it required a deep knowledge of the team and industry that wasn't easily gained. I should have taken more time to understand what was needed and what success looked like. It was utterly exhausting. I was very concerned about my reputation. If I messed this up, would it erode my credibility that I'd built over the years?

Eventually the project ended and though I successfully delivered for the client, it was a wake-up call. I could choose to take projects outside my brand, but should I? They were a slog, and they were uninspiring. Why invest precious time and energy in work I didn't want to add to my portfolio? From that point forward, I was careful to choose work that aligned with my brand because every project builds on itself.

Now, it's your turn. Let's define your ideal contract. Think back to the personal brand work you did in Chapter 3. Let those discoveries be your guide.

What are you great at? What's effortless for you? What are your strengths?

Next, recall your professional success stories. What were those moments of greatness when you were on top of the world? What was it about that role and that work that fueled you? What attributes and skills did you need to be successful?

Now look ahead of you. What problems do you want to solve? What do you want to stand for? What kind of work do you want to dedicate your time to?

When I worked in corporate America, I didn't think much about how to market myself. I was head down, doing my job, navigating office politics, and doing all the things you do to stay relevant and advance your career in a matrixed organization. However, when I struck out on my own as a consultant, it quickly became clear that I had to shift my perspective and stand for something so clients would think to hire me. I couldn't be everything to everyone. I needed to focus on what I loved. At that fork in the road, I saw lots of different paths I could take based on my experience. But which was the right one? And how would I know?

I began experimenting. I took time to think about the work I had done, which elements I enjoyed the most, and where I felt confident and engaged. I realized that I loved supporting sales and marketing teams in partner organizations and had worked in these groups for so many years that I felt confident in my ability to deliver success. I also wanted to work with people I liked and respected. That was a big deal to me, because I value relationships. So, those were the projects I sought out.

Slowly, project after project, I built my portfolio and personal brand. I had always taken a consultative approach, so being a consultant felt natural to me. I saw myself as a strategic doer. While I could do the strategy, I also enjoyed doing the work. And my clients loved that I could do both. Soon, I became known as the go-to expert for helping big sales organizations create new revenue streams and adding a sales perspective to the marketing organizations. I also built a reputation as someone who loved to coach and guide younger employees and help them manage their work more efficiently. Every project built my confidence and strengthened my personal brand.

As I shared in my story above about the project that I shouldn't have accepted, straying outside your area of expertise can have negative consequences. Now, I'm not saying that you can't expand your horizons and take on work outside your brand. Of course, you can. But ask yourself if it's work that you're excited about developing your skills. If you are, then taking on a short-term project is a great way to test your interest. You may love it and choose to pivot and expand your brand or you may learn that kind of work doesn't suit you.

It's okay to say *no*, sometimes. As an employee, I could never decline work assigned to me, but one of the advantages of being a consultant is that you get to choose your work. If you're in the position to turn down work, you can be picky. Say *no* to projects that don't light you up or fall outside your core area of expertise so that you can make space for the right ones to come along.

Ideal Contract Considerations

I like to think of this process as a funnel. At the wide mouth is your personal brand work and what you accomplished in Chapter 3. There you're defining the broad strokes of who you are and what you want to be known for. As you travel down the funnel, you're narrowing in on the specifics of your ideal project, from the work to the logistics and the client and client company.

Let's revisit step two in creating your personal brand: Be unique. Maybe you said that building websites is effortless for you. Let's get narrower still. What does your ideal website project look like? For example, consider:

Focus area: Do you want to build the whole site, soup to nuts, or focus on a particular aspect, like front-end development or UX/UI design?

Strategic or tactical: Do you want to set the strategic direction or execute against a strategy that's already defined—or both?

Tools: Are you comfortable working with the common site platforms or do you prefer to work within a specific platform, like WordPress? Do you enjoy learning new software and tools on the job or does that overwhelm you?

Familiarity: Do you want to work within a team, company, or industry that's familiar to you? Or do you enjoy immersing yourself in a new space and quickly learning what you need to be successful?

Teamwork: What team dynamic do you prefer? Do you want to work independently and share major milestones with the client along the way or within a highly collaborative team that's constantly sharing tasks and developing in tandem?

Access: How important is it to you that you have access to the team and leadership during the project? What level of support or leadership buy-in do you need to be successful?

Impact: Do you enjoy working on projects that directly connect to a big, strategic, visible initiative? Or do you find satisfaction working on projects that impact specific industries or channels?

Purpose: Do you need a project that aligns with your core values and worldview? Or is it more about delivering your expertise?

If you don't know the answers to these questions, take an educated guess. You can revise your answers as you grow into your consulting career. Get clear on your ideal contract using this list as your guide. Keep it close at hand. Use your answers as a framework to evaluate project opportunities that come your way. As much as possible, be intentional about choosing to work on contracts that align with your ideal list of considerations.

As a consultant, you choose not only the work you love to do, but *how* you love to do it. You choose what's important to you. Let's explore options when determining how work can fit into your life, so you can determine the right path for you.

Choosing to Work as a Subcontractor or Employee

As a consultant, you can work independently as a subcontractor or as a W-2 employee. There are significant differences between both options that I will explain.

Working alone as a subcontractor means that you are a business owner, not just a consultant. The good news? You are in charge. The bad news? You are in charge. You assume all the risk, and you are responsible for everything, including taxes, finances, operations, contracts, legal, business development, deployment, customer experience, and customer success of every single project. When you are your own boss, you get to choose what work you'll do, and you control everything from branding and scoping to delivery. You can choose to work alone or hire other people to grow the business.

However, the advantages of working independently can also be disadvantages. As a business owner, you are responsible for the administrative details of the business. You must allocate a portion of your time to non-billable activities including paying taxes, finding a bookkeeper, managing invoicing and collections, and finding work. For consultants who just want to do the work, these back-office tasks can feel tedious or daunting. As a subcontractor, you also forgo all the traditional perks of employment such as health benefits, 401(k) employer match, paid vacation, and more. Last, many subcontractors can feel isolated when working alone. Know yourself and consider how you work best.

It is critical to find and build a long-term relationship with a trusted accountant. They can save you money and time and also minimize your risk. They can help you establish the right business license, whether it be an S corporation or LLC (limited liability company) for tax and liability reasons. Follow the IRS guidelines to ensure you meet the criteria. When I first started my company, my accountant helped me establish my company as an S corporation. I have heard other accountants recommend an LLC structure. You may also be eligible for small business 401(k) programs, about which a good accountant can provide advice.

Don't forget taxes! The most important action you can take when starting your business as a subcontractor is to model your estimated taxes with your accountant before you do any work to manage your anticipated income. I advise these consultants to allocate about half of their earnings for taxes as a guideline. There's nothing worse than thinking you have earned a lot of money, only to find out that you have a huge tax bill you weren't expecting. You are responsible for federal, state, and local taxes, which can significantly affect your take-home pay depending on your tax rate, state where you live, and situation. Your bill rate and your take-home pay are not the same number. I know what you're thinking: *That's not fair. I earned it.* Sorry, I don't make the rules. It's better to know now, before Uncle Sam comes knocking on your door. We will go into detail on bill and pay rates in Chapter 5. For now, consider the various options for how you want to work and the resulting impact to your lifestyle and finances. Your ideal contract will allow you to work in the way that's most advantageous to you, whether you choose to be a subcontractor or W-2 employee.

Intermediaries

An intermediary is defined as a firm, agency, consultancy, or company where you are either an employee or a subcontractor. Some intermediaries hire you as an employee and place you on projects. Others provide invoice/payroll processing for you as a subcontractor or employee if you find your own work. In this scenario, you are not billing your client directly but instead through an intermediary. Many large corporations have established supplier programs with stringent contractual requirements so if you want to work for one of those clients then you will likely have to work through one of the approved suppliers, which acts as an intermediary. In this example, every supplier has a different business model and approach to what they offer consultants, so it's important to do your homework and learn which is the best match for you.

There are many advantages to working through an intermediary. For example, your skills can be aligned to their specialization, and you are part of a community. Also, they may offer benefits such as medical, 401(k), PTO, and more. As an employee, you minimize your risk as they pay the employer taxes and overhead.

Do your homework! Here are some questions to ask an intermediary:

- Will you assign me to projects, or do I find my own work?
- How do you find projects and approach business development?

- How quickly do you place consultants?
- When/how often can I expect to hear from you during the placement process?
- How do you define client success?
- What is your consultant experience? (onboarding, training and development, employee engagement, project end, redeployment, etc.)
- Do you offer:
  training and development?
  health benefits?
  401(k) plan? Employer match?
  paid time off (PTO), parental leave, and so on?
- What support do you provide during my project?
- How is my pay determined? (Hourly versus deliverable; how do you set the rate?)
- Do you offer referrals or incentives if I refer new business?
- Does my skill set align with the company's capabilities?
- How do you foster a vibrant community of like-minded professionals?
- Do you bring your consultants together for knowledge sharing and community building?
- Can you share a few references of long-term consultants with whom I can speak?

Choosing the right partner is critical to your success. Every company is different in how they approach clients, consultants, business development, social impact, margins, and so much more. Shop around. Do your due diligence and vet your options. When I meet with consultants who are shopping for the right intermediary, I appreciate their specific questions related to their needs. Your happiness will depend on your relationship with them and beyond the work and the pay, values alignment is a key factor. Your brands must be aligned, and their reputation can impact yours. If they are conducting unethical business practices, it will reflect poorly on you. I have heard hundreds of stories from consultants who have had negative experiences with companies, been bullied, received no support or transparency, and overall felt like a transaction. On the flip side, I've seen firsthand how powerful it is to work for a company that shares your values and builds a supportive community. You have a choice.

Rise of the Talent Platform

Platforms are self-service, online marketplaces that allow freelancers to post their profile and bid on work posted by clients. Platforms enable access to a global talent community that managers could not access previously. On these online marketplaces, hiring managers post a project or role, conduct their own search and screen, interview, hire, and provide project oversight. Managers can also search available talent using a variety of filters. Platforms make their money by taking a percent of the project value, usually on a sliding scale. Projects tend to be short term and smaller in scope and size. The talent is only subcontractors, so if you want to be an employee with benefits, then participating in a platform may not be a good option for you. Also, there is limited to no support helping you scope and manage your project, so you bear that responsibility.

With the rise of the gig economy and the impact of COVID-19, there are millions of people available to work on these talent platforms, making it challenging to stand out. Upwork alone estimated a 50 percent jump in freelancers on its platform in the few months after the COVID-19 pandemic hit.[2] This is where a clear and compelling personal brand becomes critical to your ability to successfully stand out and be seen.

In terms of securing consistent work, many professionals find this option challenging, but it can be a good gap filler if you are looking for small projects to augment your current workload. For those who can manage the inconsistent and short-term nature of work on platforms, this option can also provide greater flexibility.

Additional Considerations

There are a few other factors to consider when choosing how you want to work.

When: full-time or part-time? You must consider your preferences, life circumstances, and finances. Consultants like Kate choose to work part-time while their children are young. Others want to work full-time on one project with one client. Some enjoy variety and multiple part-time projects with many clients.

Where: remote or on-site? This one is a combination of the client's needs and yours. Allison only takes remote contracts because she's in Montana and her clients are in Seattle. She has demonstrated that she can do the work remotely, and the client has no problem with her being hundreds of miles away because she delivers and they can connect easily using email and Microsoft Teams. Remote work is quickly becoming the acceptable norm due to COVID-19.

How: one client or many; short-term or long-term contract? Again, it comes down to what works best for you. You can juggle multiple projects and clients, though, trust me, it can be tricky. Also, think about your ideal project length. While it depends on the work that's needed, consider how frequently you're comfortable switching gears to adapt to new clients, teams, and environments.

Choosing Your Client

Meet Alice, a worldwide event producer and another longtime Simplicity consultant. Alice's clients consistently use one word to describe her: Magical. Perhaps it's because eight of her past twelve clients have been promoted or recognized after working with her. Or because, on average, she saves her clients somewhere in the ballpark of $500,000 to $1 million per fiscal year.

Alice wasn't always a consultant. Soon after she immigrated to Canada from Taiwan, Alice was approached about transitioning from her full-time employee position to a consultant role with the same team, working remotely. She worried whether it was a step backward for her career, but she decided to make the switch and become an entrepreneurial consultant.

She likes working this way. Alice thrives on challenging projects where she can solve hard, messy problems. She consistently focuses on building her brand and maintaining her client base. When Alice thinks about her client, it's not just the person who hired her for the project—it's the whole team. She operates from a place of mutual respect in every interaction with clients and their teams and event vendors and the crew. Her successful communication and negotiation skills stem from that respect and earn her respect in return.

I love alliteration, so Alice's recipe for client success really spoke to me: passion, patience, and persistence.

Passion. In any field, you have to be passionate about the work you're doing, Alice told me, whether it's negotiating hotel room blocks for corporate events or creating data visualizations to analyze event performance.

Patience. Really listen to your client: Learn their working style, understand their challenges, and earn their trust. It takes time, but it helps them recognize that you're there to help, not take their job, and it benefits your problem solving.

Persistence. "It's an endurance game," Alice said. Track your wins and metrics and focus on the positives to keep you going during those frustrating times.

Alice views herself as an entrepreneur. And as an entrepreneur, she can choose her own path. A big part of that choice is the ability to choose with whom she works.

"I always get good clients," she told me with a smile.

Good clients show respect. They value her skills and expertise and see her for what she is, a highly skilled expert. To clients, Alice's value is readily apparent, as evidenced by her steady pipeline of projects.

After more than a decade operating as a small business of sorts, her definition of success has done an about face. She has found a niche that allows her to work for people who respect her and recognize her worth. Being seen in that light is important to Alice because she doesn't see consulting as a step back in her career—it *is* her career. She's found her personal definition of success, and that, to her, is magical.

What to Look for in a Client

Contract work isn't just about doing the work, it's also about with whom you are doing the work. All the consultants I interviewed for this book expressed that the latter is one of their top factors for accepting or rejecting a project. But what makes a good client? And what attributes contribute to the ideal client for you? This chapter will answer those questions by establishing key characteristics to look for. We'll start with Rob.

Rob was my first client. I'd worked with him for years at Microsoft. He was a vice president when I was a director, and I respected and admired him greatly. Most important to me, Rob and I shared similar values of integrity, trust, and client focus. He was entrepreneurial and valued my strategic expertise and knowledge of the business.

When I was ready to return from maternity leave after my second son, Rob seemed like the perfect client for my first project as a consultant. He had an idea for a new revenue stream but didn't have anyone on his team who had capacity to focus on defining the strategy. It was the perfect first project for me. As a consultant, I could focus on the deliverable and develop a winning strategy. My plan was not only implemented, it also expanded into a global, multiyear program that generated an additional revenue stream for Microsoft and its partners.

In hindsight, I chose my first client wisely. Working with a client I knew and who knew me helped build my confidence as a consultant. It also contributed to my success.

Rob knew me and my capabilities, so I didn't have to "sell" my skills to him. Although I never reported directly to him, we worked together in the same group for many years and knew each other well. This familiarity made it so much easier for me to deliver results because we had already established trust. Plus, I was passionate about helping the company's partners be successful. The client and the work were a perfect fit for me and my brand.

One of the greatest benefits of working on contracts is that you get to choose your clients. This was very empowering to me. In my corporate job, I didn't get to choose for whom I worked, and in many ways my career path was beholden to my manager's support. As a consultant, I loved choosing projects where I could work with people I liked, respected, and wanted to help be successful.

Your ideal client is someone who values you and respects your work. Rob was mine. Let's unpack what that means for you.

They're in Your Fan Club

We all have a network. Colleagues you've worked with over the years. Friends in the same industry or sector. Professional organizations you belong to. Contacts you've made at networking events or tradeshows. Peers in your space whom you follow and engage with on social media.

Start by identifying the people in your network who know your skills. Think about people you like, who are doing work that is interesting to you and who know your reputation. The list doesn't have to be long. In fact, shorter is better to start.

They Share Your Values

You have your fan club. And in earlier chapters, you've defined your personal brand and identified the work that you love to do. Understanding the marriage of those things is key to intentionally selecting clients who share your values. It's also key to your success, as my story with Rob illustrates.

Think about companies you admire. You likely share their values. For example, as I previously shared, if you are passionate about the environment, you may be attracted to Patagonia as a mission-driven organization that considers the stewardship of our planet a top priority. Perhaps the company's leadership style or code of conduct is important to you. Or maybe you want to work in an environment where innovation, challenging the status quo, and disruption are celebrated and encouraged. Whatever it is, define the values you want represented in your client's company and identify which, if any, are nonnegotiables.

Get clear on what cultural elements are important to you, too. Do you gravitate to a relationship-oriented environment where teams are collaborative, friendly, and open? Or do you prefer a quiet, analytical, and focused environment? Do you want to work with a team that clocks long hours and expects near round-the-clock availability, but rewards itself with frequent happy hours and socializing, or a team that works hard, but respects work-life balance?

Once you determine what values matter most to you, examine your prospective client's team and company through that lens. You can usually get an intuitive feel for the culture when talking to employees and reading anonymous online reviews.

Whenever possible, reach out to people in your network who have worked either as employees or consultants with your target client companies. Schedule short, fifteen-minute, informational calls to ask them about the company and what they like and dislike. Do your due diligence to ensure you are entering a culture where you are set up for success.

When Deanna, training and development expert, took a project with a high-growth ecommerce client, she found herself in a culture that didn't distinguish between full-time employees and consultants. It wasn't obvious that she was a consultant by her email address or signature, and they made her feel like an integral part of the team. When they went out of their way to include her, it not only felt good, it also provided the knowledge sharing she valued to help do her work better.

Company Size Matters

The size of the client's company also matters. Maybe you're very comfortable in the bureaucracy and complexity of huge corporations or want to work alongside a team of other consultants. Or perhaps you thrive in smaller companies where you can wear multiple hats and work directly with the founder. It's a personal choice. There is no right or wrong answer. Figure out what works best for you.

Large companies tend to have more secure budgets and potential opportunities, but they also have more processes, rules, and hierarchies to learn and understand. Small companies usually operate at a much faster pace because there are fewer people and processes blocking decision making, and people working within small organizations generally have more ownership and responsibility.

Remember Keri, the marketing strategist for startups? When she first started consulting, Keri looked to the obvious places for contract work: the successful enterprise organizations in her local market. She was consistently landing projects, but the work didn't inspire her. When she started taking on small business and startup clients, she knew she had found her niche.

Smaller companies—startups in particular—need Keri's passion for strategy and scale. She loves to dig in and solve big, meaty problems and create strategies and processes where none existed before. Her voice is heard, and she's often able to work directly with the C-suite. She thrives on owning entire pieces of the business strategy, giving organizations the true foundation for success, and then getting out. She can't make that same impact or tap into those same internal passions for a client at a large global company.

But startups don't always make it, so it can be risky. When they don't succeed, especially when you're paid in equity, not cash, then you don't get paid. And smaller budgets and smaller teams can result in Keri's least favorite part of consulting, which is chasing down payments.

"Years ago, I purposefully pivoted my company to focus more on the startup space," she shared with me. "But as you can imagine, that comes with some volatility and financial risk. I love that my big Fortune 500 clients always pay *and* pay on time, but I find the fast-growing, recently funded business space to be more dynamic and personally rewarding, so I take on that risk. But it sometimes comes at a cost. Companies don't always survive. Sometimes they lose funding, and sometimes they just have poor leadership. I hate playing the collection agency."

Keri has learned to work in a very specific corner of the startup space: well-funded ventures that need a full marketing strategy, and bonus points if they're led by a dynamic, driven CEO. Those companies have the runway to pay for her services, yet they have the high-growth and high-impact qualities she's looking for in a client.

Do Your Due Diligence

As is true when you're interviewing for a traditional role, as a consultant you are evaluating your potential client as much as they're evaluating you. Before you agree to a project or even meet the client, ask around to backchannel check their reputation and level of respect.

To Kate, the writer and executive communications consultant, the client trumps the work. It doesn't matter how cool the project is, if she doesn't like the client, she won't take it. She'd rather work on a mediocre project with a great client than the other way around.

Whenever possible, Kate does some reconnaissance before pursuing a project or stepping into a meeting. Once, she found a project that sounded amazing on paper, but when the first two people she asked about the client both led with "Well, . . ." that was enough for her. Their hesitation told her everything she needed to know. She didn't pursue the project.

And when you do meet with the client, learn to screen for character, and trust your gut.

Kate says you can tell a lot in an interview, whether it's virtual or in person, by the questions they ask, how they ask them, and whether they're interested in you as a person.

If you pick up on red flags that indicate their disrespect and you're in a position to turn down the work, do so.

"I have a pretty solid 'no assholes' rule," says Keri. Every time she hasn't trusted her gut after that initial meeting, she regretted it as soon as the project began.

Now that you have identified your ideal contract, let's talk money. You will learn the art of the rate and how to determine yours in Chapter 5.

Reflection Questions

Let's build your dream project.

- Do the work you love . . .
    What is your personal brand?
    What are your strengths and passion?
- However you love to do it . . .
    Do you want to work part-time or full-time?
    Remote or on-site?
    Alone or through an intermediary?
    As an employee or a subcontractor?
- For whom you like . . .
    What are the values of your ideal client?
    What companies do you admire and want to support?

FIVE

MASTER THE
ART OF THE RATE

"Know yourself. Know your worth."
—ANONYMOUS

I ENTERED THE BUSTLING CAFÉ ON a cloudy Seattle morning and looked around for the person I was scheduled to meet.

I'd landed my first contract as a consultant, and my client asked for my bill rate. I had no idea how to think about my fee and needed to learn stat! *What should I charge for my services? How should I structure payment terms? What do I do if the client doesn't have the budget? Will the client think I'm worth it?* And it wasn't just that I didn't know how to think about my pay, I felt awkward asking people to pay me. As a former corporate employee, I'd rarely needed to talk about money or negotiate my pay. Now, as a consultant, I needed a crash course in understanding my value and setting my rate range. I needed to get comfortable with confidently pricing contract work based on my expertise and asking for what I deserved.

A former colleague suggested that I reach out to Tom, a successful strategic consultant, for guidance. While I had never met Tom, he and I had both worked in corporate and risen through the ranks to director-level roles. I was hopeful that his perspective would help inform my market value. And here I was at the café, ready to get some pointers. I spotted him and gave a wave of recognition. I ordered a latte, and then made my way to his table and sat down.

After we exchanged pleasantries, I handed him the details of the strategy project I had been awarded.

He gave it a once-over and, with confidence said, "We have similar backgrounds, and I'm charging $25,000 a month for strategic work."

My eyebrows rose in shock, but I kept my thoughts to myself as I took notes appreciatively. It seemed like a lot—too much, even—but was that just my insecurity talking? *Could that be my market value? Could I really charge that?*

Taking the last sip of my coffee, I thanked Tom for his time and left, my mind racing a hundred miles an hour. *Could I really bill what he suggested? Were my experience and skills that valuable?* The number he recommended seemed high, but I had nothing to compare it to besides my own salary. When I sat down at home to do the math of calculating my consultant market value based on adding my previous salary and fully burdened costs as an employee, I began to realize how many costs a consultant incurs and that the bill rate is not the same as the pay rate. Once I calculated my fully burdened cost as an employee and compared it to my consulting bill rate, then I began to see that the numbers were within reach based on the work I was doing at the current market rate.

That conversation in the café gave me the confidence to pitch my rate—the one that made my eyebrows shoot up to my hairline—to my new client, Rob. I approached the conversation with a matter-of-fact air of practiced confidence. I shared my market research on the nature of the work with Rob. Being that it was a strategic three-month project to create a new revenue stream, and based on my level of experience—here it comes—the monthly cost for this work would be $25,000. I stopped talking and waited for his response.

Rob seemed to be doing the math in his head and considering his budget. I waited with anticipation. Then he said: "Great, let's get started. Will you draft the statement of work so I can get the P.O. open?"

I tried to hold back my excitement. "Of course," I told him. "I'll have that to you by the end of the day." I thanked him for the opportunity, firmly shook his hand and quickly departed his office with a grin on my face that reached from ear to ear. I had done it! With each project, my confidence grew as I worked hard to demonstrate value and justify my price tag. I learned to believe I was worth it and that my skills had value.

Let's talk about everyone's favorite topic: money! If you're anything like I was, you have a lot of questions. You might be wondering: *Do I bill hourly or by deliverable? How do I know my market value? Am I getting paid enough? Did I set my number too high or too low? How do I calculate my rate? How do I know my client will pay me?*

I call this chapter "Master the Art of the Rate," because determining your bill rate and pay rate as a consultant is an art, not science. Many factors influence the right number for you, and they may change over time. Money is just one part of the equation. A host of other highly valuable intangibles are difficult to place a price tag on.

We will explore all aspects that contribute to determining the right fee for you. By the end of this chapter, you'll understand the basics of rate, know how to set your range, and have a firm grasp on your worth. My goal is to give you the knowledge to go out into the market with confidence and earn what you deserve for your skills, experience, and the work. You've got this.

Rate 101

Let's start with the basics, including the difference between bill rate and pay rate.

Your **bill rate** is what the client pays you or the intermediary on your behalf. If you bill a client directly as a 1099 subcontractor, then your bill and pay rate are the same. If you work with an intermediary, they will include a fee for their services. Depending on the intermediary's level of transparency, you may or may not know the bill rate to the client, and the intermediary may only communicate to you your pay rate.

Your **pay rate** is what you get paid, either directly from an intermediary or from the client. This is not your **take-home pay,** because you have to deduct taxes and other costs depending on if you are a W-2 employee or a 1099 subcontractor. If you are a W-2 employee, you will need to set your desired tax deduction and pay taxes, whether you elect to have them deducted from each paycheck or pay them at tax time. If you are a 1099 subcontractor and own your business, then you will need to deduct additional taxes and overhead to determine your take-home pay.

As a rule of thumb, I advise subcontractors to put aside roughly half of what they bill for taxes and other costs. It's a conservative estimate, so even if your taxes and expenses don't end up equating to half of your pay, then you will appreciate the buffer. For example, if you bill a client $10,000 a month, then as a 1099 subcontractor you should expect to allocate about $5,000 each month for taxes and other expenses. Over the years, I've heard stories about consultants who don't plan appropriately for tax day and are shocked by the imminent tax bill. That usually only happens their first year, and then they become good savers.

The bottom line is to seek wise counsel from a good accountant and understand your tax liability before you quote your bill rate. If you aren't sure whether you want be a W-2 employee or set up your own business as a 1099 subcontractor, a good accountant is invaluable to help you run both models with your current financial situation so that you can make an informed decision. Paying an accountant up front to help you understand your tax liability and more is a small investment that can save you a lot of money and headaches down the road. To find a good accountant, ask other consultants or business owners with whom they work and if they have found their services valuable. Not all accountants are created equal, so be sure to talk to at least three, and make sure you understand what they are saying. The relationship with your accountant is one of your most important business relationships, so you need to feel comfortable that this person has your back and connects with you. I found my longest-term bookkeeper-turned-accountant after going through four different ones. In the early days, I didn't check references; I took people at their word. That was a mistake. Take your time, check references, make sure they are credible, and work with other business owners like yourself.

Contracts can be structured hourly or deliverable-based, depending on the nature of the work. Either way, it's critical to detail in the project's SOW (statement of work) the work you will complete, including end date and rate. Hourly contracts are paid by the number of hours you work, which can fluctuate based on the project. Billing terms can be set weekly, monthly, or by milestone. Deliverable-based contracts are calculated based on the work promised, as detailed in the SOW. Billing for deliverable-based contracts can be invoiced and paid weekly, monthly, or by deliverable milestone.

If this seems confusing, please don't panic. In this chapter, I'll share a few sample calculations to help make it real. Over time, especially once you get a firm handle on how to think about your market value and your worth, this will become second nature.

But first, let's talk about mindset.

Approach Your Rate with Confidence

As I mentioned before, determining your rate is an art. As with any artform, it requires a certain mindset to achieve the desired effect. To successfully set your rate, you must step into it with confidence. To do that, you must believe in yourself and know your worth.

Believe You're Worth It

Kate, the writer and executive communications consultant, admits that she does every textbook example of what women do when determining what to bill.

When she was approaching one of her early projects, she came up with a rate that sounded reasonable to her. She asked her husband, a real estate agent, for a gut-check reaction, and he was shocked.

"No!" he said. "Go in at the highest rate!"

She demurred, but he was resolute. "Don't leave money on the table," he said. "Start at the absolute highest amount."

That was the pep talk Kate needed. She went back to her consultancy and asked about the client's rate ceiling.

"Okay," she said, when they told her. "That's my rate."

Kate was certain the client would balk at the price tag and counter with a lower number. But they didn't.

"They didn't even blink," she said, shaking her head. "I thought, *Why am I undervaluing myself? How much money would I have left on the table?*"

That's how Kate has approached the money conversation ever since. She starts at the highest amount and sticks to it, although she still second guesses herself every time.

And when the client blinks? If they truly don't have the budget or don't need someone as experienced, she walks away. Alternatively, Kate suggests a creative workaround like working fewer hours on the project, either by working part-time or completing the work in a shorter period of time.

But usually, they don't blink.

I have coached thousands of people over the years, mostly women, and I've seen Kate's initial reaction play out again and again. When it comes to money negotiations, many, but certainly not all, women tend to undervalue their experience and not ask for what they deserve. PayScale reports that 31 percent of women are uncomfortable negotiating their salary, compared to only 23 percent of men.[1] And according to a 2020 compensation report from Randstad, a global staffing firm, 60 percent of women have never negotiated their salary—much higher than the 48 percent response from men.[2] Let me say this: You are worth it. I'll say it again: You are worth it! Remember that. Believe that. Own that. If you never ask, then the answer is always no.

If, like Kate, it's difficult for you to ask for what you are worth, there are a few strategies for building the confidence to ask for what you want. First, take the time to educate yourself on your market value. I will review this in detail in the next section. I find that data is an important factor for believing in your worth. It's the evidence that reveals your market value. Also, ask yourself what's the worst that will happen when you negotiate for what you deserve? Do you think the client will laugh in your face and tell you you're not worth it? I've never seen that happen. Either they will say yes because they know you are worth it, or they will offer an alternate rate, which you can decide to accept or not. Either way, you win.

Know Your Market Value

Many ever-changing data points determine your bill and pay rates.

While no one source is perfect, it's helpful to use free and transparent tools to build an informed pay estimate. Online resources, such as PayScale, Salary.com, Glassdoor, or Indeed, will help you get a sense for what someone with your skills earns in your local market. For example, I like to start with an online search for a generic title in my local market, such as "marketing manager salary in Seattle." The search may reveal a broad range of salaries. While this isn't perfect, it does provide visibility into local numbers for that type of work, and you should immediately see a spectrum start to take shape. I usually do several searches with a variety of titles based on my experience to educate myself on what the market is paying.

Then, to really get a good handle on what market rates are for your skills, talk to people you know who are doing the kind of work you want to do at your target companies and inquire about their salary range. You can also apply for positions and go through a traditional interview process to learn about their pay ranges. Every city is different, and it's important to do the research on a consistent basis to ensure you are being paid fairly and that you have a pulse on the market.

You are collecting multiple data points to help you form a realistic expectation for your bill and pay rates. It's important to conduct this exercise every couple years or so, as local markets change. You may also see that the market and what you need to earn are at odds. This discovery may motivate you to research which high-demand roles pay more and proactively build your skills in another area.

Market value is always top of mind for Young, a business management consultant. He is a numbers guy, and he's brilliant at making them understandable to non-math types and using data to tell a gripping business story. Perhaps it's no surprise then that Young has mastered the art of the rate. Clients value his expertise so much that they revise budgets and prioritize his contract just to secure his services. He has commanded a premium fee for more than a decade because, quite simply, his clients love working with him.

Young takes great pride in his work. Since he started consulting with Simplicity Consulting in 2008, he's always had work. Clients find him based on his reputation for excellence. Every single one of his clients has gotten promoted. Young uses that as his scorecard.

"If I do my job well, they're going to do well and shine within their team," he told me in a video chat. "Every time they get promoted, it's an opportunity for me to reinforce that I helped their success."

Though Young knows his worth and is confident in his ability to deliver successfully, he's careful to view his services through the lens of the client. "It's like buying a car," he explained. "Why would someone select you and not someone else?" He benchmarks himself against the market and others with similar skills and expertise.

"You have to always ask yourself: *Am I marketable?*" he continued. "*Are there automations, efficiencies, or trends I should know? Are people in my role providing different services because of advancements in tech? Should I teach myself to use those tools?* You need to understand where the market is going."

That knowledge of the market and his place in it has paid dividends for Young. It has allowed him to navigate his career at his own pace. It has also allowed him to stand firm in his worth and hold strong to his rate. You can, too.

Value Your Intangibles

Money is important, but there are so many other factors to consider when taking on a project. I call these the *intangibles*, and everyone places different value on them. Intangibles include work schedule, logistics (such as remote, on-site, or hybrid), the people you work with, the skills you learn, the company, and networking opportunities, to name a few.

What are the top intangibles for you right now? What considerations—anything other than money—factor into your decision to take a project or not? For me, it was freedom and flexibility. After the birth of my second son, I placed a huge premium on working flexibly and controlling my work schedule. In fact, those intangibles were so important to me that I quit my corporate job to achieve them.

Your Work Is Not Your Worth

We are talking a lot about money in this chapter and the intangibles around the money that are of value to you. It's important to take a human moment to recognize that your worth is not directly tied to your work.

Our society has an underlying narrative connecting your work and your worth. It's easy to be seduced into thinking that if you're loyal to an employer and give your blood, sweat, and tears to an organization that you will be taken care of. But it's not true. The reality is that you must find your definition of worth and know that it has nothing to do with your title and job. Sadly, many people are devastated when they get laid off without seeing it coming. They have tied their identity and their worth to their work.

Your worth is about who you are as a person, regardless of your current role or title. I remember having a mini identity crisis when I first left my job. At Microsoft, employees have a blue identification badge, and my email alias was lhufford. These things are so culturally significant that employees are referred to as "blue badges," and consultants are identified by their orange badges. I didn't realize how attached I was to my alias until I was no longer a blue badge. If I wasn't lhufford, who was I? My identity and self-worth had become so intertwined with my work that I was attached to an email alias. I felt a little off-balance but realized I was not alone. Over the years, I've met many people in similar circumstances grappling with losing their work email alias.

I got over my attachment by focusing on opportunity. I realized that on this new path, I could create a new alias and definition of success for myself. That inspired me, and I hope it inspires you, too. That is the power of disconnecting your work from your worth and opens possibilities beyond your wildest imagination.

How to Determine Your Rate

Now, it's time to talk specifics. Your rate is based on several factors, including your skills and experience, market value, and the scope of the project. Let's start with determining your pay range.

Set Your Pay Range

A pay range allows you to accept the right projects based on your low and high rate requirements. Identifying your pay range will empower you to feel in control of pricing and give you the confidence and flexibility to know you are getting paid what you deserve and desire.

To calculate your pay range, you must first decide if you want to work as a W-2 employee or a 1099 subcontractor. As a W-2 employee, your pay range includes employer taxes, benefits, and overhead, so your pay range would be lower than a 1099 subcontractor. If you are a 1099 subcontractor, your pay rate is the same as your bill rate (less any intermediary fees, if necessary) because you are responsible to pay for all additional taxes and expenses from your business.

Next, let's identify your baseline, or low, and your ceiling, or high, by evaluating several factors.

We'll start with your baseline. First, determine how much you need to live, including your rent or mortgage, insurance, car payments and gas, childcare and schooling, cell phone and internet, utilities, entertainment, savings, taxes, incidentals, and any other foreseeable expenses. If you don't already have a monthly budget, take some time to review your bank statements, credit card spending, and bills to create a budget. You can find a good financial planner to help set your budget, and there are many great budget-tracking apps, such as Mint, to help you stay on track. All set? Great, you've calculated your baseline! This number represents the amount you need to live. Your baseline is your "can't go below" amount at the low end of your range.

To determine the ceiling of your ideal pay range, you need to understand your market value for the work you can deliver based on your experience and expertise. If you are a professional leaving an executive corporate position, then you likely have a history of a higher salary and pay expectations which would be commensurate for similar strategic contracts. The high end of your range must be supported by prior work you have done to command a higher rate for additional similar work.

Now that you have your baseline and your ceiling, you have your pay range. This is a huge step. This range will help you be intentional about the work you want to take and when to say no. It will give you the flexibility to vary your workload and know that any amount within your set range will allow you to pay your bills and maintain your desired lifestyle. It will give you the confidence to take roles that you're super excited about even though they're on your lower end of your range, or to quote a number that at first seemed too high, but you now know is within market value and meets your financial requirements.

Determine the Right Bill Rate for Each Contract

Once you know your pay range, you have the foundation you need to negotiate your bill rate for a given project. Let's get into the nitty-gritty.

Option A: Find your project and invoice directly with your client: When you directly invoice your client as a 1099 subcontractor, your bill rate and pay rate are the same. Remember, your pay rate is not your take-home pay.

Option B: Work through an intermediary who finds you a project: If you work through an intermediary that places you on projects, then you won't have to negotiate directly with the client. A portion of the intermediary's fee includes their negotiation on your behalf. They will take this burden off your shoulders, and you only need to communicate your ideal pay range. They can also inform you about current market pay rates for your level of expertise, which can influence your pay range.

Option C: Find your project and bill through an intermediary: You land a project through your network and are required by the client's supplier policies to work through an intermediary for invoicing. If you choose to negotiate your bill rate with your client, remember to build the intermediary invoicing fee into your bill rate so you don't absorb that cost. Different companies include the fee in different ways, so be sure to ask how your intermediary does it and, most importantly, document everything in writing.

Every contract has unique expectations, deliverables, and dependencies that influence the bill rate. To set the right bill rate for each project, look at both sides of the equation: What you want and what the client wants. Your desired number is based on your financial goals and the range you calculated. The client's needs are usually set by their budget and how they value the deliverables.

The Work Dictates the Rate

Not all work is created equal. As a consultant, your rate represents the value of the work as determined by the client. Many factors contribute, including the client's budget, whether the work is tactical or strategic in nature, and your expertise.

I have coached many senior, strategic consultants who can command high sums for a combination of strategic work and their expertise however sometimes clients don't need all their capabilities and view a contract as more execution than strategic. It may have nothing to do with your value, and it's a personal choice if you want to do work that may be easy for you. This approach does not dilute your brand or rate for future work.

Especially when you're first starting out, I recommend expanding your options. Consider a range of projects from the tactical to strategic, and open yourself up to more opportunities. This is where your range becomes valuable. For example, you may be approached to do a project that is easy for you and on the low end of your range, but you determine it's worth it because the intangibles outweigh the money.

Remember that you have control over the work you do and the range you set for the level of that work. I have seen consultants take on multiple clients at varying rates depending on the work. If it's easy work for them, they like the client, and they have the bandwidth, consultants can be more competitive with pricing. If the project is ambiguous and hairy, they can charge more, because they know it will take more time.

I had this experience as I began consulting and was approached by a client who wanted me to fix a problem. It was messy. I knew it would be long hours, and I was uncertain about my ability to deliver success. But I love a good challenge, and by this time I had completed a few projects and developed my confidence. I proposed a number at the high end of my range, thinking that the client didn't have the budget, but, low and behold, they hired me. I was glad that I factored in the extra work and pay because, though success ultimately prevailed, the project was a beast. Had I billed too low, I might have felt resentful about not getting paid for the extra work. Nothing is worse than expecting the project to be tactical and pricing it on the lower end to find out that it's much more strategic and time consuming and that you've billed it too low.

Compare Apples to Apples

It's safe to assume that most clients will look at your bill rate and compare it to their salary. They may do this unconsciously, so don't be surprised if you hear comments like, "Wow, you get paid a lot." Many don't understand that their employee salary is only one component of the fully burdened overhead cost to the company that employs them. If a client says your fee is expensive, this is a great opportunity to educate him or her on the difference between a consultant's bill rate and an employee's annual salary.

When helping the client accurately price a project, you can share your learnings about the market based on your research. The fully burdened cost of an employee varies from company to company, depending on the costs companies incur on behalf of their employees, and ranges around 25 to 50 percent above the base salary. This accounts for employer taxes, benefits, 401(k), office, equipment, and all the associated overhead.

In order to provide a meaningful market estimate, I like to share an apples-to-apples comparison. Let's say an employee's annual salary is $100,000, and the company attributes a 50 percent burden cost for its employees. The fully burdened cost of that employee would be the salary ($100,000) plus the burden cost (50 percent = $50,000), for a total of $150,000.

Although employees know they have these benefits, they often don't include these extra employer costs as part of their total package when comparing themselves to a consultant's bill rate. As a consultant, your bill rate can be more or less equivalent to the fully burdened cost of an employee for similar work.

The client is not responsible for paying the consultant's overhead and risk as they would if you were an employee. However, someone has to pay those costs. Either you will have to pay for your own taxes, benefits, and other overhead as a subcontractor or the intermediary you work through will pay those costs for you as its employee. The bill rate is inclusive of all costs, regardless if you are a W-2 employee or 1099 subcontractor.

Finally, help the client view the work at the level they need, and then compare it to the market. For example, strategic work at a C-suite rate demands a much higher range than tactical project management work.

Know Your Range, But Stay Open to Opportunity

Let's say you're offered a project at $6,000 a month, the very low end of your range. However, it comes with all the flexibility you need and for a great client at a company where you want to build a network. Would you take it? For some, the intangibles outweigh the gap between your range's floor and the client's budget. For others, it's truly all about maximizing earnings. It's a personal choice, but for most people, it's about so much more than just money. Of course you need to be paid enough to make a living. I'm not suggesting you give your services away, however, I do encourage you to think about all those other things around the money, the intangibles, that contribute to your happiness and success. What if you can build new relationships in a company that you are excited to work for? The short-term, lower rate may justify this investment to have the opportunity to prove yourself for future, higher-value work.

How to Set Your Rate When You Want to Change Industries

I worked with a consultant who was passionate about video games but didn't have work experience in that industry. Travis was an avid gamer; he wanted to translate his project management skills from a different industry to the one he was passionate about. He decided to take an opportunistic approach and take any contract at any pay that gave him a foot in the door. He valued having the opportunity to prove himself and expand his network and build relationships with people in the industry. He was confident that, if given the chance, he could demonstrate his enthusiasm and ability to successfully deliver, enabling him to navigate to other future opportunities. For Travis, taking on a junior project management role—despite the fact that he was a senior resource—was worth it to gain critical industry expertise and make connections. The work was easy based on his past experience, and the rate fell at the very low end of his range, but it made sense for him because his current motivation was the opportunity, not the pay. He landed a project in his dream video game group and worked hard to prove himself and build relationships. Based on his successful track record, he was offered high-impact contracts allowing him to flex his experience muscle and earn higher compensation for the work he loved.

Sometimes You Just Need to Work

The realities of life dictate that sometimes you just need to work even if it means saying yes to a project that doesn't inspire you. I realize that this contradicts everything we've been talking about regarding your personal brand and doing work you love and that is meaningful. However, I get it—I'm a practical person. Although I believe that we should strive to do work that aligns with our strengths and passions, we also must pay the bills. If you find yourself in this place, acknowledge it. Don't get down on yourself if you take a role that you aren't thrilled about, but don't stay there forever. Give yourself a timeframe and create a plan for how you will continue to pursue the work you love. Sometimes it takes a while to find those perfect roles. Don't give up! Work your plan and keep on the hunt for the work you love. Don't wake up miserable one day because you stayed far too long in a project that you weren't passionate about.

I have seen consultants wrestle with their ego and self-identity around taking work that they view is beneath them. This is a very personal decision; however, I can assure you that, as a consultant, nothing is beneath you. Every project is an opportunity to learn and develop new skills or continue mastering what you know and, more important, build your network. You never know whom you will meet and where they will end up next. If you show up as someone who made an impact, people will remember you and happily refer future clients your way.

Pay Expectations Over Time

Many consultants expect an increase in their pay over time because they have a traditional employee mindset. This is not how consulting works. You are paid for each project as the client has defined the value of that project work. Many people are confused by this as it is a different way of thinking about your pay for the work you do.

If you want to earn more, then you need to build your skills in an area where the market is paying more. You cannot expect to get pay increases as a consultant for doing the same work. The work has been scoped by the client at a specific rate, and if the work stays the same, then there is no reason for the client to increase the pay. If the work has changed and you are doing more work that the client values, then there is an opportunity to present your additional work as above and beyond and re-scope the work at a higher rate. The client may or may not agree with the additional work you are doing or see value in it but it's worth having a conversation.

Remember: You are worth it. Your work is not your worth. You now have the skills to ask for the rate that aligns with your market value. I hope that this chapter gives you the knowledge to set your pay range with confidence, factoring in all the intangibles that are important to you. In the next section, we'll explore successful nego-tiation strategies.

And just like that, you have built your foundation! You defined your personal brand, complete with your authentic words, success stories, and a clear, compelling personal brand statement. You identi-fied the ideal work, work environment, and client for you. And now you know how to think about pay rate and bill rate. I hope you are feeling confident and credible. If you aren't, then review Part II again and focus on the questions that are unclear for you. Take as much time as you need to build your foundation. Don't rush it. You are creating a strong root structure to support you.

In Part III, you will use your newfound knowledge to spring into action. I'll show you how to build your flywheel momentum—from landing the contract and delivering excellence to carving out time to reflect and refresh. Here we go!

Reflection Questions

- What is your ideal pay range?
- What is the market value (bill rate) for your skills/ expertise?
- What intangibles are just as important to you as money?

PART III
The Flywheel

SIX

LAND YOUR CONTRACT

"Whether you think you can or think you can't, you're right."
—ATTRIBUTED TO HENRY FORD

" **I** T FELT LIKE I WAS wearing a life jacket, and I'd been thrown in a lake of molasses," Christopher, a business strategist, told me. "I'm not going to drown, but I'm sure not getting anywhere very fast."

He was in his late thirties and had been managing a team of fifteen or so with a $20 million budget at a large tech company. He'd always loved the work, but in the ten-plus years he'd been there, the culture was starting to change. It just wasn't very fun anymore, and it was harder to get things done.

He wanted an opportunity to play a more significant role by helping a business thrive and grow. So, he took the leap and left his secure corporate job for what he believed was going to be a career-defining opportunity. Christopher had spent a few months negotiating an advisory role for a late-stage startup with considerable venture funding and a solid customer base. The company wanted to test a new indirect-sales business model, led by Christopher. He'd repeatedly stressed to the company's board that, to be successful, this couldn't be a short-term project. It was at least a year and a half, maybe two.

"Of course," they assured him. "We're committed to this thing."

Yet when Christopher arrived at the office on that first day, something was off. The vice president of human resources was there for his initial onboarding meeting, along with an acquaintance who had first connected him with the company.

Then they broke it to him. The CEO and CFO had resigned the day before. They couldn't share any details, but he was definitely out of a job. Christopher couldn't believe the news. The role he'd pinned his hopes on—the one he'd left his comfortable corporate job for—no longer existed.

Christopher was stunned by the sudden turn of events. He sat down to a blank piece of paper and started writing. By 10:00 a.m., he had a list of a hundred or so names of people he knew from his former job. He figured he'd start by reaching out to the first twenty and see where that took him. By the afternoon, people were already responding.

It was a Tuesday in the fall of 2008. By Thursday, Christopher landed his first contract. That same week, the Dow dropped 1,800 points. He felt fortunate to have found a stop-gap contract to provide income while he looked for something more permanent. *This is just temporary,* he thought. *Something to pay the bills until I find a real job.*

That "real job" still hasn't come along.

Life happens. Sometimes, when you need options and fast, it happens in ways that you never see coming. Fortunately, contract opportunities move quickly, too.

Let's move into action, so you can land a contract as fast as you need. You're in the home stretch! You have completed the foundation, the heavy lifting, and the necessary internal work to find a contract. You understand what work you love, who your ideal client is, and how work can fit into your life right now. All your effort will prove to be worth the results, because you will stand out with a clear, compelling personal brand that is authentic to you.

In Part III, we set that foundation in motion with your flywheel. If you recall, the flywheel is built on this consulting truism: Great work leads to more work. All the actions outlined in this section— landing a contract, setting yourself up for success, delivering excellence, and reflecting and refreshing—add momentum to your flywheel. Each successful project, client referral, and new connection power its rotation. Your activities can and will give you the momentum needed to land your next gig.

This chapter will give you the tools to create and land a contract rather than relying on someone else to find it for you. Even if you feel uncomfortable finding your own work right now, I encourage you to try these strategies in addition to building relationships with recruiters at staffing and consulting companies and agencies. This two-pronged approach will increase your odds of finding contract work. Create as many options for yourself as possible because you never know where your opportunities will come from. Sometimes they will come directly from your network, other times from a friend of a friend or a recruiter. How quickly you land a great project is directly related to your level of activity.

Confidence, connections, and credibility are essential to land work you love. You gain those things by building a personal brand that energizes you, intentionally cultivating relationships, and doing great work. Regardless of how you came to contract work, whether you planned to become a consultant or it accidentally happened to you like it did with Christopher, these core strategies will increase your chances of landing a project doing the work you love. To find the right project for you, it all comes down to telling your story consistently everywhere, working your network, and managing your mindset.

Tell Your Story Consistently— Everywhere

You already defined your personal brand. Now, put your personal brand into action. Landing your first project and setting your flywheel in motion are all about consistently telling your personal brand story often and everywhere.

When I say *everywhere*, I'm talking about all the platforms and ways that communicate who you are and what you do to the world. That includes your LinkedIn profile, résumé, personal website, blog, or online portfolio, if relevant; references and testimonials; and any other social media accounts, such as Twitter, Facebook, and Instagram. It also includes how you talk about yourself, which influences how others talk about you. Though you'll customize your messaging based on the platform and the audience, each touchpoint should ladder up to a consistent personal brand story. Here I'll walk you through how to tell that consistent story across channels, both online and in person.

If you don't already have a LinkedIn profile, build one. It's the first thing employers and clients look at. Did you know that almost 40 million people have been hired by someone they connected with on the platform?[1] Think of your profile as your résumé on steroids. It is the standard for professionals, and maintaining a standout presence

is critical to being successfully found and seen as a credible professional. Even if you are a student or recent graduate who is just starting
out, create your profile now and add to it as you go. It's a living and
evolving story of your professional life and brand.

As you acquire more skills, you are in control of how you represent
yourself and determine how you want to show up in the world. You
get to choose your professional picture, background, thought leadership videos and presentations, and the work experience to showcase.
You're in control of who you want to connect with and how to build
your network, from thought leaders to colleagues and peers. In our
virtual world, a robust online profile makes it easy to continue to
develop the relationships that you want.

Because LinkedIn is so ubiquitous, I recommend starting there.
Once you build a powerful profile, copy, paste, and customize it for
other formats, including your résumé. Whatever you say about yourself on your profile, make sure that it tells a cohesive story from your
headline and summary statement to your background pictures and
media highlights.

Profile headline: Grab your audience's attention with a catchy,
compelling headline. Make sure that it reflects who you are and what
you want to be known for. You can include your title or your authentic words. Think beyond your title or area of expertise. What phrasing will make you stand out? For example, rather than lead with
project manager, you could say *I make order out of chaos*. Here are a
few examples of headlines that stand out:

*Communication Strategist, Storyteller, Speechwriter. Writing, elevat-
ing, and amplifying narratives to change the world.* This headline from
Catharine, the storyteller you met in Chapter 3, beautifully states
what she does and the impact of her work.

Social storyteller, communications professional, and curious optimist. A former colleague's headline demonstrates his area of expertise, while offering a glimpse into his personality and worldview.

Working at the intersection of culture & communication to build learning and development content, DEI programs & employee engagement. This consultant's headline encapsulates the work she does that wouldn't be conveyed in her title.

Brand & marketing strategist for early stage companies. You don't have to overthink it, either. Take this example from Keri, the marketing strategist for startups we've met previously. Her headline briefly and clearly states her expertise and focus area.

Summary statement: This is your About section. The descriptive text block where you can expand on your headline and go into more depth about who you are, the impact you've made, and the work you're looking for. Think of this as your extended personal brand statement, not your résumé highlight reel. This is the place to include any notable results, awards, or other things that make you unique. For example, here's a snapshot of mine:

My mission—and the reason I founded Simplicity Consulting—is to help everyone thrive in the new world of work. When I started Simplicity Consulting in 2006 after the birth of my second son, I wanted flexible work that still added value and leveraged my skills. Today, I'm proud to be founder and CEO of a company that helps talented experts do they work they love, while helping busy managers achieve their goals faster.

Building businesses is my passion. After fourteen years managing and growing strategic multimillion-dollar accounts for corporations, I embarked on this journey to help people find significance and success at work. I love facilitating the matchmaking process, from coaching professionals who choose to maximize their expertise and transition to project work to helping companies understand how to leverage on-demand experts to drive impact.

My first book, *Personal Brand Playbook*, offers five simple steps to transform your unique skills and passions into a clear, compelling personal brand. My second book, *Navigating the Talent Shift*, teaches managers how they can easily build on-demand teams and get faster results.

Profile picture: Keep your picture professional, while being true to your brand and your industry. LinkedIn reports that a professional profile image yields fourteen times more profile page views.[2] What's considered professional varies by industry and function. For example, a collared shirt and suit may be the answer for someone in the finance industry, while a more casual look and an infusion of personality may work for a creative designer or photographer.

Background image: Find an image that supports your brand. My current background image is a picture of the Seattle skyline with our company mission statement emblazoned across it, which represents where I live and my company. Get creative with your background image as this is an opportunity to show your personality and make a memorable first impression.

To put it all together, let's look at Catharine again. Her profile picture is professional without being overly formal or stuffy. Her background is a modern black and white image of a microphone, which represents her public-speaking clients. The work experiences at various companies she's listed, along with the teaching she's done, consistently tell the story of her focus on storytelling and communications, which supports her headline. Her educational experience includes a degree in communications and relevant courses she has taken. In a less-than-ten-second scan of Catharine's LinkedIn profile, you clearly know who she is and what she stands for. She has painted a consistent picture of who she is professionally and personally through her words and images.

Remember your high school English class? The paragraph structure you learned in the classroom, pairing a thesis statement with topic sentences, also works well for your profile. Think of your headline as your thesis statement. What do you stand for? What are you about? Then your experiences, or topic sentences, should support your thesis statement. What was your primary impact in that role? What were you responsible for? What professional success story best supports your overall personal brand or thesis?

Your profile shouldn't be an exhaustive list of everything you've ever done, with no rhyme or reason. It should tell a consistent story with an intentionally curated narrative. You may choose to deemphasize certain work experiences, because they don't strongly support your headline. That is perfectly fine. You can list jobs with dates and a simple summary of your accomplishments. Then for your other work experiences that do support your personal brand, you will elaborate on those and showcase your success stories, results, and contributions. These will stand out as a reader skims your profile.

Once you've got that dialed in, customize that powerful story for your résumé and other online touchpoints. Ask a friend or colleague to review them when you're done. At a glance, are they all telling the same story? Is your personal brand clear and compelling? Are they clear? Do they convey what you hoped? If you are a marketing generalist and want to focus on attracting social media marketing work, does your headline and work experience tell this story or does it still look too generic? Continue to ask yourself these questions often, because your profile is never done.

Take the time to thoughtfully build your profile *before* you reach out to prospective clients. If you quickly create a profile in ten minutes, those people who consider you for work may be unimpressed with your limited online presence. Put yourself on the path of success and be proud of your profile before promoting it. You are evolving just like your personal brand, so take the time to update your headline, reach out to people you've worked with to ask for testimonials and attach examples of your work or thought leadership that support your brand.

Your story isn't confined to the written word. Telling your story *everywhere* includes how you introduce yourself and describe your work in conversation. Whether it's a brief chat in a coffee shop or an introduction at a networking event, the words you say about yourself matter. Use them as another opportunity to put your personal brand into action. Dust off your authentic words and your personal brand statement. Rehearse the highlights of your success stories. Consider and practice the language you'll use to introduce yourself and talk about the work you've done and want to do. You have the power to tell your story with clarity and intention. Embrace that power.

Work Your Network

The flexibility of consulting has enabled Deanna, the training and development expert, to pursue a career coaching business for recent graduates on the side. In her coaching, Deanna helps newcomers to the work-world identify the kind of work they want to do and instills the power of networking. Every single consultant I spoke with for this book echoed the importance of networking.

Deanna follows her own advice about networking consistently, not just when looking for work. She keeps in touch with contacts in her network when she comes across news or updates that they'd find interesting. For example, she recently sent a note to a former client when she heard of a new e-learning platform. It prompted a quick virtual demo-date for them to test drive the new tool. It may not lead to a new project, but that's not the point—it cultivates a meaningful relationship that's fulfilling and mutually beneficial.

When you land that new project or role, she says, send a quick note to update anyone who helped you along the way. It's a great excuse to reach out, and it shows that you appreciate their help and value the relationship beyond just what they can do for you.

Ask for Referrals and Introductions

When it comes to referrals, "Never make the person across from you work harder," Deanna cautioned. That's why I stress the importance of telling your story clearly and consistently, so it's easier for others to remember and retell it. It also helps to provide the person you're asking for help with a clear, concise description of who you are and what you're looking for, so it's a lighter lift.

Rupali, a communications strategist, always asks for new connections, even when she's not actively looking for work. To continuously expand her reach, she asks everyone she speaks with in her network if they know of anyone else she should connect with. It's as simple as tagging, "Is there someone else you recommend I talk to?" to the end of every conversation. Rupali makes clear that in this introduction, she's not asking her network to simply recommend her for a job.

"You don't want to put them on the spot, and ask them to say, 'She's looking for a job,'" Rupali said. "That shouldn't be your first goal with anyone."

Instead, she frames her ask around a specific question or perspective.

"It's more about the guidance," Rupali shared. "'I'm really interested in what you're doing. Can you give me some guidance on how you structure your communications team?'"

When she is looking at a potential project, she always tries to find a link between the client and her network. A good word from a mutual connection goes a long way in opening the door and building that initial interest with a potential client. She also recognizes that it's a two-way street and looks for ways to return the favor in the future. This reminds me of the power of the law of reciprocity and always looking for ways to do something nice for others.

Reframe Networking as Relationship Building

I have met very few people who enjoy networking. It can feel disingenuous and exhausting, and at its worst, it's a confidence killer. And yet, networking is incredibly important. Consider this statistic from LinkedIn: Referrals are nine times more likely to get hired than non-referrals.[3] It's time to reframe your perspective on networking. Take the pressure off yourself. It's not about you. It's about building relationships, getting curious, and determining how and where you can add value to other people.

Rupali loves networking for this very reason. She has reframed it as connecting with others. "I love connecting with people," Rupali shared with me. "I love listening to their stories, learning about what they're going through, getting their advice and guidance, and finding ways I can help and support them."

Rupali approaches networking as an ongoing process. "Don't just reach out when you need something," she said. And when you do, think of it as a combination of organic and planned outreach. For example, she sets aside thirty minutes a week to reach out. "Set a goal for yourself, whether it's weekly or monthly," Rupali advised. "Otherwise it's one of those things that will slide."

Remember that you're not asking for a job. You're not there to sell anything. You're there to listen and learn. Be an investigative reporter, ask good questions. Try to understand their challenges and perspectives. Then follow up with a thank-you email and specifically what you learned from them. People who give you their time want to feel that they've made a difference and helped you. Show your gratitude, and it will go a long way.

As an outside observer of Christopher's consulting career, I am most impressed by his ability to maintain a consistent project pipeline, despite not actually soliciting work after that first project. While he doesn't consider himself a "good" networker, he does believe in the old adage, "You've got to network to get work." Christopher focuses on consistently maintaining good relationships, one lunch at a time.

Let's deconstruct The Lunch.

While he's still on a project, months before he needs to start looking for his next project, Christopher will schedule lunch with a former colleague or acquaintance.

Invariably, the first thing out of their mouth is, "I really don't have any projects for you."

"That's okay," Christopher will assure them. "I'm chock full. I can't take anything on right now."

And because he's genuine in his response—he's truly not looking for work in the moment—their defense comes down. They'll catch up and talk about life and work.

And sometimes in that same lunch, his acquaintance will be talking about work and realize, "You know, I do have this thing. Do you know anybody who can help me?"

Or maybe a few months later when they have something, they'll call Christopher to see if he's available. All because he goes in without an agenda and doesn't just reach out when he needs something. He is focused on building a genuine relationship and not expecting anything from that lunch except to cultivate a positive relationship.

We can learn a lot from Christopher's successful strategy. First, he is a true professional with a great reputation in his area of expertise with many fans and success stories. Second, he genuinely cares about the work he delivers and wants to make a positive difference. Because he is so sincere, his authentic approach to building relationships focuses on helping rather than selling. Always keep the client and the client's needs front and center. This is the secret of great consultants. They realize it's not about them, it's about their clients.

Plant a Lot of Seeds

When you're looking for a contract, think of yourself as a farmer. To harvest a bounty, you need to plant seeds. A lot of them. Every day. Consistently. And those seeds can take a while to grow. You never know which seeds will grow and which will wither and die, so just plant seeds. The more seeds you plant, the more you increase your potential for opportunities.

Treat looking for work as your job. Set a structure and consistent schedule for your days. When Cassondra, senior business program manager, is looking for her next contract, she treats it like just another day at the office. She wakes up at the same time, showers, dresses professionally, does her makeup and hair, and maintains the same start time each day. Between then and her set end time, she focuses on connecting with her network and looking for opportunities to add value. This structure helps her stay focused and confident in her ability to ultimately land a contract.

Ready to try your hand at planting those seeds?

Think back to the ideal client that we discussed in Chapter 4. To recap, your ideal client is someone who values and respects you and your work, knows what you're good at, shares your values, and possesses the cultural and environmental elements that you're looking for.

Now, back to Cassondra. She prioritizes values alignment when she's looking for her next project by sorting prospective clients into an A and B list.

The A list consists of people who share her values, mostly work friends and people she recently worked with who know her and her skills. She prioritizes outreach to her A list because she knows that the work relationship will be more enjoyable, and the work output will be successful. She's in relatively close contact with folks on this list, so she's comfortable reaching out to them with a coffee invitation to say: "I'm rolling off my project soon. Do you have any projects coming up or do you know anyone who does?"

The B list are people she worked with in previous years and/or work acquaintances she doesn't know well. With them, she takes a less-direct approach via email or social media: "Hello, just checking in . . .". She puts her feelers out and stays top of mind without coming on too strong.

It's your turn. Take out a piece of paper and create two columns. Label them A and B. You are going to make your list work for you by working your list, just as Cassondra and other successful consultants do. The goal is to sort your network into those two categories of possible clients. Do not prejudge anyone and don't overthink it. Complete the lists as fast as you can. It's always good to have more people to contact than you need. This will help you feel like you have a good pipeline and options even if you won't need to reach out to all of them.

A List: This is a list of people you know and like. They are part of your personal fan club, and they know your work and your greatness. You have skills they want on their team but aren't sure if they have budget or a business need. If they don't have contract work for you at the moment, they will happily go out of their way to refer you to others in their network. This list doesn't have to be very long, because you only need one person to hire you at a time.

B List: This list is a mixture of acquaintances with whom you have had limited interaction as well as new companies and clients. For the former, think about people in your network whom you suspect share your values, but you're not sure if they have any contract work available. For the latter, consider companies or clients you don't yet know anything about.

Once you've built your lists, it's time to take action.

Start with your A list. This is where your reputation and credibility matter. Once you have your list, craft personal emails to your top warm leads. Share that you are available for your next project and provide a short description of your personal brand and your expertise. You are not directly asking for work because that could be a turn off. You are sharing your status and placing yourself on your fan club's radar in the event there are open projects. Remember, these are the people who find joy in helping you. Often, the people closest to you have no idea you're looking for work, and they would readily hire you to help them or refer you to someone else. I see this common scenario with people who are leaving their corporate jobs and just starting to look for their first project. Just like the example of Christopher, once you begin to share with a small group of people who know you and your greatness that you are on the market as a consultant, they may be thrilled to have you help them.

Your B list will require more care and feeding, but don't overlook its importance. Building relationships online from a cold network *is* possible, and this is where the power of LinkedIn really shines. For example, let's say you are a product marketing manager who wants to do more of that kind of work. You can search LinkedIn for other product marketing managers and even filter for your target companies, location and more. You can see your network connections and learn who is connected to each other.

To make those connections, you can either ask your mutual friend to make a warm introduction or reach out directly with a short personal note. If you're asking for an introduction, follow Deanna's advice and don't make the person you're asking work too hard. Clearly articulate your request and add an equally clear and concise description of who you are and what you're looking for. Do the heavy lifting for them and provide language that they can literally copy and paste into an introductory email.

For those connections that you initiate, make your introduction as personal as possible. Do you have a specific person, college, or previous employer in common? Are you both marketing or engineering leaders? Find a common connection and share it so that the recipient knows your intent. Sometimes I connect with people on LinkedIn who I admire and appreciate the work they do and that is what I share with them. The most important thing is to be authentic and genuine in your intent. No one likes to feel like they are getting an impersonal spam request. Your response rate may not be very high, but don't focus on that. Just focus on the activity. You are planting seeds, remember? You are looking for the right person, and you only need one to respond. Besides, it's always a no unless you ask.

Sometimes No Means Not Right Now

I want to take a moment to talk about rejection. Nobody likes it. Hearing no after you put yourself out there can be exhausting and demoralizing. Over time, it starts to chip away at your confidence.

Consider reframing the word no. You will hear no more than yes—it helps to know this before you start. Try to gamify the process. Give yourself a goal: How many noes you can get? What about forty? Fifty, even? You will probably land a project before you hear that many, but now you can see each no as getting you closer to your goal.

Remember, you only need one yes. That's one project and client that you're excited about. Looking for that takes time and patience. Focus on building relationships and offering value. Doing so will make you memorable. Later, when those noes *do* have an opportunity, they may reach out. Sometimes no simply means not right now.

You Only Need One

As Dale Carnegie says in his book, *How to Win Friends & Influence People*, we hire people who we know, like, and trust. You must do the internal work to build your confidence and to represent yourself as someone who will add value and be helpful and not a desperate job seeker. You don't need the whole world to hire you, just the right person. One at a time. You are trying to find that person who needs what you have to offer.

You never know where work is going to come from. You must consistently share your personal brand which is another reason it is so important. If you're really clear about your expertise and value, you will eventually attract the right person to hire you. The hard part is not knowing when that will happen. But it will. Hang in there!

Put Yourself in the Client's Shoes

As you look for work, it helps to put yourself in a prospective client's shoes. They're busy, stretched thin, and often have gaps in skills or resources on their team. Managers usually have way too much work and not enough time or resources. And they don't need just any help, they need the right help. What's more, many managers struggle to find the time needed to grow their employees' skills to the next level.

When you look at things from the client's perspective, it's easier to see the value you can add. As a consultant, you solve an important problem for managers. You make their lives easier and better. You're an expert who focuses on a specific deliverable that they won't have to manage. Frame your outreach with prospective clients through this lens. Use that perspective so you can pivot to add value based on what the client needs and wants. As you are planting seeds, demonstrate how you can make the client's life easier while helping them achieve heroic success.

It's on you to be proactive with your outreach. Hold yourself accountable for maintaining the relationship and checking in with them when you say you will and offer value. You don't want to be annoying, but you do want to be visible. Think of ways to add value or offer your expertise via email or by following them on social media and commenting. I like to share relevant articles with prospects that I think they will find interesting to show them I'm thinking about them.

Rupali, the communications strategist and networking devotee, wears her client hat to land a contract. She draws on her former corporate experience and focuses on being proactive and meeting the prospective client halfway.

"I remember being in their position and thinking, 'If I just had another pair of hands.'" Rupali said. "I show them that I can do that, that I want to help."

Often the prospective client is so backlogged with work that "they haven't even thought it fully out," Rupali told me. "They just know that they're overwhelmed."

She brings that perspective, along with some initial research on the company and client's specific business, to their very first conversation and every interaction thereafter. She outlines their problem, how she can help solve it, and throws in a few suggestions for other areas she can help that the client hasn't considered yet.

"It's part art, part science," Rupali added.

I love Rupali's story because she understands the key to landing a project which is showing the client how you can solve their problem and help them reach their goal. Get inside their head. Understand what they're thinking, and what keeps them up at night. Demonstrate how you are uniquely qualified to help. Show them how you have the knowledge and skills to help them be successful.

Create Opportunity

Rupali also stresses the importance of being proactive and not simply waiting for a project to knock on your door. In her conversations with her network, she anticipates potential opportunities by asking the right questions and drawing on her experience.

For example, Rupali had a client who she really hit it off with. They had a great working relationship and built a friendship, too, so when the client moved out of state they kept in touch. When her client moved back to head the communications department for a new company, Rupali was already in touch with him, so reaching out didn't feel desperate or one-sided.

In their conversations, Rupali began to see the areas where her former client was struggling and had immediate ideas for how she could help. Though neither of them knew at the start whether there was a project there, over the course of a few months, Rupali was able to demonstrate how she could add value. She positioned herself to help her former client build out his team and set up his entire department for success.

The initial project turned into a subsequent project, and even resulted in a full-time job offer. Rupali turned it down, she's too committed to the consultant lifestyle, but turned that offer into yet another contract. All because she used her subject-matter expertise to ask the right questions with a relationship that she intentionally nurtured over time.

Your Mindset Matters

A positive, resilient mindset can move mountains. Ground your approach in an attitude of gratitude in every interaction and at every twist and turn. Remember you are offering your value in the spirit of helping. As you launch into creating and landing your ideal contract, think of every opportunity as a chance to learn and grow. Bumps along the way are inevitable. Keep going as they are a part of your learning process, and they happen to everyone. Reframe setbacks as improvements that will help you get closer to your ideal project.

Let Go of Things You Can't Control

Your ability to stay positive and keep moving forward is directly related to your activity in those areas that you can influence. You cannot control when someone will call you back, or has time to meet with you, or whether those in your network will refer projects to you. You cannot control a company's internal budget process or hiring policies. Don't focus your energy on things outside your power. If you do, your confidence will suffer, and you'll start telling yourself stories that aren't helpful. You can choose the words you say about yourself, how you represent yourself, both online and in person, whom you reach out to, how you respond to obstacles, and how you take care of your body, mind, and spirit. Be intentional about keeping your focus on those things that are within your realm of influence.

You also cannot control when the right project will come your way. Stay the course. Focus on consistently building relationships over time, especially when you don't need work. Stay present and focused on today while allowing yourself to look ahead to the next six to twelve months. Stay open and positive and continue to do the work, one conversation at a time. Those conversations will help you learn, and you never know where they will lead. Always ask if there is anyone else they recommend you talk to. This is how you build your network and relationships through your warm referrals.

Jim Rohn, an entrepreneur and motivational speaker, popularized the notion that you are the sum of the five people you are around most often.[4] Take a moment to reflect on who those five people are for you. Are they positive and uplifting, or do they tear down your hopes and dreams? Do they stretch and support you or encourage you to stick with what is safe and easy, even if that jeopardizes your happiness and fulfillment? You need a fan club that believes in you and what you are doing. It's really hard to work this way if you don't have a support network. Find your people and choose to spend time with those who care about you and your success. Intentionally make time for these people in your life, and stop making time for the negative ones.

Stay Positive

Choose positivity over negativity. Embrace positive people, behaviors, habits, and actions every day. We are constantly being influenced by something or someone, even when it's unconscious. It's so easy in our media-driven culture to turn on the news and become depressed in five minutes. Understand your limits. Observe how you feel after scrolling on social media or watching TV or YouTube. Do you feel better or worse about yourself? Chances are that the answer is worse. A recent study funded by the US National Institutes of Health (NIH) concluded that participants who used social media the most were nearly three times more likely to be depressed than those who used it the least.[5] Does it look like everyone else has it figured out? News flash: They don't. Social media only offers a curated view into a tiny sliver of people's lives, so you only see the good stuff. Become aware of those activities that build you up and make you feel good after and do more of those.

Keep Swimming through the Peanut Butter

Landing work can feel hard at times. I liken the process to swimming through peanut butter. It's thick, opaque, and a bit sticky. It's difficult to see, and it's challenging to navigate. When you're swimming through the peanut butter, you begin to question yourself.

Can I do this? Will I ever make it out? Why is it so hard for me to see the path ahead?

Take a breath. This is not the time to have a pity party for yourself. It's the time to roll up your sleeves and revisit your personal brand. Ask yourself if there is an area of expertise that you want to expand on. For example, if one of your skills has less demand than you thought, do you have other more marketable skills that you could emphasize? Do you want to broaden your pay range and open yourself up to more opportunities? Do you need to expand your network and push yourself out of your comfort zone? There are many factors that go into creating and landing a contract, and you are in control of turning the dials on the process. Just keep swimming.

Finding a contract takes patience and persistence. Don't give up. Keep going until you find the right project for you. Remember, focus on what you can control, stay positive, your mindset matters and keep moving forward even when it feels like you're swimming through peanut butter. You are making progress every day. Keep telling your personal brand story, build relationships and plant seeds. It will pay off and it gets easier with each contract that you successfully complete. Create opportunity for yourself by looking for problems that you're uniquely qualified to solve.

Eventually, you'll find a client with a great contract, and hear those magic words: They want you! . . . Now what? Next, set yourself up for success.

Reflection Questions

- Is your LinkedIn profile current? Do your picture, headline, work experience, and testimonials clearly showcase your personal brand?
- Are you actively cultivating your prospective client A and B lists?
- Do you have an attitude of gratitude? Are you looking for ways to add value and help others as you plant seeds?

SEVEN

SET YOURSELF
UP FOR SUCCESS

"Doing the best at this moment puts you in the best place for the next moment."

—OPRAH WINFREY

T ALK WITH HEIDI FOR JUST a few minutes, and it's clear that she is great at what she does. She has been a business strategy consultant for the better part of her career, and she thrives on turning tough, complex challenges into structured and successful programs.

Heidi has identified a few basic truths for consistently delivering excellence. And it all hinges on how you start.

"'Start as you intend to go on.' That's something my mom always said to me. I remember when I had my first baby, repeating that mantra over and over and over," Heidi told me. "Don't go into a project thinking, 'We'll adjust this in the future,' because that's not going to happen.

I set clear boundaries in the beginning. They are kind, but really clear."

She sets all her projects up for success by establishing kind, but clear, boundaries early on building trust from day one, and modeling direct, open communication.

"I'm here to help you," she tells her clients. "My goal is to make you look good."

Her approach has paid off. Heidi is highly sought after by clients, and she commands a high bill rate. Her success is grounded in part on how she starts a project. Heidi's mantra, passed down from her mother, is reminiscent of the second of Stephen R. Covey's *7 Habits of Highly Effective People*: Begin with the end in mind.

> Begin with the End in Mind means to begin each day, task, or project with a clear vision of your desired direction and destination, and then continue by flexing your proactive muscles to make things happen.[1]

At Simplicity, we put it another way: How you start is how you finish. I stress this with consultants and clients alike. No matter the phrasing, I can't emphasize this enough: start strong. Set clear expectations upfront. Get clear on the work and what success looks like for the client. A strong start is the key to successfully delivering on your project.

In the previous chapter, after working your network and putting your personal brand into action, you identified a project opportunity. Here, we'll move that opportunity through to the project start. You'll learn why it's so essential to begin with the end in mind, from scoping the project and negotiating your rate to creating a detailed statement of work (SOW). It's the little things that make a big difference between good and great consultants. Take the time to establish clear expectations from day one. It's your responsibility to take this action, not your client's. If you are working through an agency or intermediary, they should provide this support for you to ensure your mutual success. If you are working independently, follow these steps to set yourself up for success.

Scope the Work

Don't just allow the client to send you a bulleted list of tasks or deliverables. It's essential that you have a conversation, ask questions, and adequately scope the project work.

Schedule a meeting with the client. It doesn't have to be anything overly formal. Give the client a chance to outline specific business needs and use it as an opportunity to demonstrate how you think and communicate. The goal is for you and the client to walk away with a clear and shared understanding of the project's scope, the problem that needs solving, and a high-level view of what success looks like for the client. Be sure to frame the conversation around the defined project at hand as it relates to your specific skills.

If you're already familiar with the client and the business, this is often more of an organic process. If it's a new client in a new-to-you business or industry, add more structure to the conversation. To prepare, research the client and the team, company, and industry. Jot down a few thoughts on how your expertise maps to what you understand as the problem. Identify specific examples of how you approached similar projects and the resulting outcomes, successes and failures alike. Prepare a list of thoughtful questions that will help you dig deeper into what the client needs and what success looks like for them. Bring energy, demonstrate active listening, and pretend that it's your first day on the project. You are an expert, and you have what it takes to solve the client's problem.

Take a consultative approach. Ask enough questions until you can clearly articulate and define success and how you will deliver it. This conversation will give you the information needed to draft a comprehensive SOW for the client.

Over time, you will customize these scope conversations based on your working style and your relationship with the client. These standard questions—spanning business basics, project specifics, budget, logistics, and timing—are a good starting point.

Business Basics

Get a better understanding of what the client does and what their success metrics are.

Questions to ask:

- Can you provide a high-level view of your role, what you do, and how you/your team contribute to the company's mission?
- What does success look like for you? What success metrics are most important to you?
- What are your business goals? What are your most pressing challenges?

Project Specifics

Ask detailed, probing questions to get at the problem(s) they're trying to solve and better understand what's in and out of scope for the project.

Questions to ask:

- What specific deliverables do you need?
- What are the due dates and milestones?
- Why is the project needed now?
- What do you foresee as the biggest challenges?
- Whom will I need to work with on this project? What additional stakeholders, if any, are required to sign off on this work?
- Are there any meetings relevant to this project?
- What skills and experience are necessary for this project?

Budget

It can be awkward to talk money, especially at first, but *please* don't make the mistake of avoiding budget in this conversation. You need to know before investing any more time and energy that the client's budget aligns with your pay range.

Question to ask:

- What budget do you have in mind for this work?

Logistics and Timing

Get a handle on all the project logistics. Address as many of these as possible in the scope conversation. If you run out of time, send a follow-up email with a consolidated list of open questions.

Questions to ask:

- What are the project start and end dates?
- Will I work remotely or on-site? If on-site, do I need

building access; how many days per week; and where should I sit?

- What are the expected working hours or times to be available (or propose your ideal work schedule)?
- What tools does the team use? Do I need special network access to any internal portals or tools?
- Will I be issued a company laptop or am I expected to use my own?
- How do you prefer to be communicated with (email, in person, chat/messenger, phone, etc.)?
- What day works best to schedule a weekly (15–30 minutes) one-on-one meeting where I will review my status on the deliverables?
- What stakeholders, teammates, or vendors will I need to interface with?

Don't leave this meeting until you can articulate the client's problem and how you will solve it. Paraphrase what you heard the client say and talk through how you would approach the work. This will help you confirm your understanding of the client's needs while allowing you to demonstrate your approach and gain the client's trust. You want to feel aligned and in sync with the client. If you don't, then continue to ask questions and reframe how you would solve their problem. Tread carefully if you don't clearly understand the desired outcome of the work, because usually when it's not clear up front, it's unlikely to become any more clear later.

Negotiate Your Rate

Once you have a clear sense of the project scope, deliverables, and the client's budget, you can set your rate for the work. View your pay range through the lens of the project specifics and market value for the type of work and determine your number. Remember to account for taxes, fees, and other deductions. See Chapter 5 for a refresher on mastering the art of the rate.

I recommend a deliverable-based pricing structure and a monthly invoicing schedule with a clear start and end date and rates by milestones. This approach manages everyone's expectations about the work that needs to get done. If the work is ambiguous then define the outcomes over a period of time, such as three to six months and bill a flat monthly amount. If you bill hourly, set a not-to-exceed amount, and expect to share a detailed breakdown of your work with the client.

In this section we'll explore common rate roadblocks, and how to overcome them.

Request for Proposal

Sometimes clients need help pricing a project. If they want you to provide a proposal, it's a great opportunity to educate them on your knowledge of the market, their specific needs, and your skill set. Make some informed assumptions for the client and consider the fully burdened cost of an employee to do the work as a data point to justify your rate. It's an imperfect science, but a valuable data point.

For example, let's say that the work as described by the client sounds like something you could hire a marketing manager to do. Based on your research, annual salaries for marketing managers in your local market range from $80,000 to $120,000. For the sake of this example, we'll assume an average $100,000 salary, with an estimated total cost of a fully burdened employee to the company of roughly $150,000. Then ask the client if that estimate is in the ballpark. Whether it is or isn't, you acquire important information. If your calculation is accurate, you can estimate a monthly cost of $12,500; that is, $150,000 annual fully burdened salary divided by twelve months, as a data point for full-time work. If you are billing the client directly as a subcontractor, this monthly amount is both your bill rate and your pay rate. If you are billing through an intermediary, you must add those fees (typically 10 percent) to the bill rate, so you don't unexpectedly absorb that cost. If you are working part-time, take the appropriate percentage as a guideline to help establish your rate. For example, if you are working twenty hours a week, cut the full-time rate for forty hours a week in half to determine your rate.

Don't Wait to Talk about Rate

I strongly advise you to discuss budget in your initial scope conversation with the client. Early on in my consulting career, I didn't. Like many people, I had a hard time initiating a conversation about money, so I waited until the last minute. I ended up wasting time and frustrating both myself and the client. Set your comfort aside. Talk about money upfront and get specific.

Here's where I went wrong. I found a project that seemed like easy work, but I spent far too long working with Janie, the client, to define the work and results before discussing budget. It wasn't until a few weeks later, when we were about to start the project, that I shared my rate. Janie was shocked. When she disclosed her budget, it was a mere fraction of my rate as a senior consultant. The chasm seemed too wide to use a creative workaround, and I felt terrible.

I turned the project down. It wasn't the right fit for my skills, and if I had taken it at the budget, I would have felt taken advantage of and likely become resentful. But most important, I lost Janie's trust. Because I wasn't forthcoming about my rate from the start, she assumed that I was going to do the work regardless of her budget. In hindsight, I should have better managed the situation. From then on, I always discussed rate in the initial conversation and with confidence. If the clients couldn't afford me, I didn't waste their time or mine. And if I knew someone who was a better fit for the project, I was happy to refer them.

Creative Contract Structure

The client's budget may fall short of your desired pay range. Get creative. This doesn't have to be the end of the contract. You have options.

1. **Carve off a piece of the work and offer to do that chunk for their allocated budget.** If the client truly doesn't have enough budget, you could start by completing a portion of the work, ideally something with a high chance of success, to gain the client's commitment to the project. Doing so will help connect you with future opportunities, possibly even the remainder of the work.

2. **Work part-time or fewer hours on the project for their available budget.** Again, it doesn't have to be all or nothing. Propose working on a subset of the project, either in a part-time capacity or for fewer hours overall to maximize their budget while maintaining your market value.

If there's just too much of a gap between their budget and your rate, politely decline and, if you can, recommend someone who may be a better fit. This is especially true for strategic consultants with a high bill rate. Clients may want your expertise but can't afford you because the work as scoped is less strategic and more tactical. If you turn down the project, pay it forward and recommend others in your network whose skills and experience level are more aligned. This is a win-win-win. If your referral gets the project, he or she will remember your generosity and will likely reciprocate at some point in the future; the client has found the right resource; and you feel good about helping others.

Client Won't Share Budget

Sometimes, when you ask clients for the budget, they may turn it back on you: "I'm not sure. What do you bill?" As with the request from proposal example above, this is another great opportunity to share your knowledge and educate them on the market value of the work they need done.

Also, don't feel like you have to respond immediately. You could simply say, "Let me process what I learned about the project and your business needs in our conversation today. I'll put together a proposal for you based on what I've heard and price the work appropriately for my skills and market value and give it to you by tomorrow. Will that work for you?"

Important caveat: If you're a high-billing consultant who's firm on your rate, then be transparent. If you never, ever go below a certain number, tell the client that when you're asked. You'll save a lot of time and heartache this way.

Sticker Shock

Heidi, the business strategist from earlier in this chapter, weighs a combination of factors when negotiating her rate, including her years of experience related to the project, the market, and the pay she'd receive in an equivalent position as an employee (factoring in any employee pay bands that may exist at the client company). If a client pushes back on her high bill rate, Heidi asks a few questions to get clear on the level of expertise that the client truly needs: "Do you have the bandwidth to handhold someone? Or do you want someone senior who can really take this on and take the work off your plate? Do you want to be shielded from the headache that's involved in getting the work done?"

It's most important to help a client scope the appropriate level of resource needed. If you are a strategic consultant, explain your value and how you will help them.

"Because they're not going to get a senior person at a junior rate," she said to me. "If the client wants a senior person who not only can do the work, but also manage interactions with internal and external stakeholders, they know they have to have someone who doesn't need babysitting and can just do the work."

Sometimes, they won't need a resource with your level of experience. That's okay, too. You can choose to politely turn it down and refer someone from your network.

Competition or Doubt

If the client isn't fully convinced that you have the right skills or experience for the work or they're weighing other options, bring forward your personal brand success stories. Show them how you've solved similar challenges and the outcomes you achieved for your clients.

If you really want to work for the client, consider creating a proactive proposal. Outline the client's problem and sketch out, in broad strokes, your recommended solution. It will give the client an opportunity to see how you think, and if you're truly in business development mode, it will help you stand out. Very few people go above and beyond.

Someone in my network connected me with a young woman named Molly. She was starting her own public relations agency and wanted advice on how to grow her business. In our conversation, she asked about our PR needs at Simplicity Consulting. I told her that we didn't currently have any budget allocated for it, but I'd be happy to review a proposal if that changed in the future.

Within the week, Molly followed up with a short, but compelling, proactive proposal. She proposed a three-month trial of a thought leadership program, complete with a few dream headlines that were customized to my business and region. It included the benefits, her process, and the cost, along with an overview of the trial program. Molly's proposal made it look so easy. She, the expert, would guide us to the promised land of dream headlines.

It's important to note that aside from the enticing slide with my company's name placed in sample headlines for premier publications in our space, Molly hadn't needed to do much. She simply made some customizations to her existing proposal template.

Ultimately, although her proposal was compelling, a PR investment was not a priority for my business at that moment. I thanked Molly for her time and referred her to a few potential clients. And when we *are* ready to invest, I'll start with Molly. Timing is everything, and Molly planted a seed with me that I will remember.

While she didn't walk away with a new project in hand, she was professional and happy to receive referrals and continue to cultivate our relationship.

Hourly versus Deliverable

As I've already shared, I recommend deliverable-based billing instead of an hourly model in most cases. It's equitable and fair to both parties, and provided your SOW is descriptive enough, you know exactly what you're going to deliver and when you're on the hook to deliver it. The client is paying for the market value of your expertise and the outcome of your work—not how many hours it takes to complete it.

However, a client may want you to bill hourly. If it's an ambiguous project without clear goals and deliverables but there's work to be done, hourly billing can make sense with set guardrails. If not, try pushing back by stating the benefits to both parties of billing by deliverable, alongside a summary of market value and the deliverables you've clearly scoped. If the client still insists, define some parameters.

Set an expectation for the number of hours you expect it will take to complete the work and make sure the budget is sufficient. Once you've confirmed the budget, set a maximum, or not-to-exceed, bill amount. This will minimize the risk of the client complaining that the bill or the number of hours worked exceeded the client's understanding, or worse, refusing to pay you for work you've already done.

For example, you could agree to bill hourly up to $10,000 before reconvening with the client to discuss what's next. An agreed-upon maximum fee will allow you to vet that they have budget to pay you and creates a natural project checkpoint to pause and evaluate progress toward the goal. If you go this route, make sure that you have something to deliver by the time you've hit the not-to-exceed amount.

If you don't have much to show for your work, the client will have a hard time justifying further investment.

Create a Clear Statement of Work

Armed with the rich information gleaned in your scoping session and your bill rate, draft a clear, descriptive SOW. This document defines all aspects of the project. It serves as the central source of truth for expectations and successful project delivery. Focus on deliverables and outcomes, not merely tasks and activities. Above all, be as clear and detailed as possible. Leave nothing to the imagination. Ensure that anyone reading the document will understand the deliverables, timeline, and path to achieve them.

Your SOW should clearly detail your name and the client's name, project description with all deliverables, and corresponding due dates, invoice terms, schedule, payment terms, and start and end dates, if applicable. Include room for your signature and the client's, and once signed, ensure that you both have a copy so you can refer to this document if things change as the project progresses. It should include enough information for you to successfully manage your time, understand your deliverables, and track your progress.

For example, let's say that you're a content marketer who's been hired to help a client with email marketing. A weak SOW may focus too heavily on the activities—sourcing, curating, editing, creating content, and scheduling and sending using a marketing automation tool—or lack sufficient detail on the desired outcomes. In contrast, a descriptive version focuses on clear, measurable outcomes, such as four email newsletters per month for six months, directed to a specific audience segment, featuring content from a prescribed list of internal teams, with targeted calls-to-action that support the team's core business goals, tracked against a list of KPIs (key performance indicators) included in the SOW. Rather than belaboring the how, an effective SOW emphasizes the what and the why to guide your efforts as an expert.

Establish Payment Terms

Once the statement of work is signed by you and the client, they will provide you with a P.O. (purchase order). Do not start any work on the project before receiving a P.O. Without it, you have no binding commitment from the client and client company to pay you for your services and you put yourself at risk to not get paid. In order to execute the P.O., set your invoicing arrangements and define payment terms.

Questions to ask:

- Can I invoice directly, or do I need to invoice through an intermediary?
- What's the process for invoicing?
- Do you have an invoice template you'd like me to use or can I use my own?
- What are your payment terms (net 30, net 60, etc.)?

You can typically bill direct at smaller companies. If your client is unsure whether you can bill direct or must work through an intermediary, they can work with procurement or their supplier team. If your project is with a client at a large organization, you will most likely need to work through an established supplier (intermediary) or become one. When in doubt, ask.

With a signed SOW and P.O. in hand, you've landed your contact. Take a moment to celebrate—this is a huge milestone! You are officially an actively working consultant. When your celebration winds down and you've downed your last sip of bubbly, it's time to get to work. Once again, how you start is how you finish. Set yourself up for success by proactively managing client expectations. You are the expert. Step into that role, showcase your expertise, and focus on enabling your client to be the hero.

Start Strong

Heidi kicks off each project by building trust and communication. She schedules a weekly check-in meeting, one-on-one, with her new clients. In her first one-on-one meeting, Heidi tells them: "Listen, I'm not easily offended. Please speak directly and freely with me." Doing so "immediately establishes a foundation of trust," she shared with me. "It's important for the clients to know that I'm there to help. I will work hard, and I want them to be pleased. And if they're not, I want them to tell me sooner rather than later, so I can change course."

She also asks two questions in every client one-on-one: "Is there anything I'm not focusing on that I should be? And is there anything I am focusing on that you'd rather I didn't?"

"I want to make sure they're happy," she added. "Asking those questions tells them that this project matters to me and making them look good matters to me. So please tell me where you'd like me to prioritize and focus."

I advise you to follow Heidi's lead and schedule a recurring weekly one-on-one with your client. Thirty minutes, you own the agenda. Bring your SOW, which should outline the key project metrics.

Create a spreadsheet or list of deliverables to share with your client in each meeting. Color code each metric, so your client can gauge the status of each item at a glance: red for blockers, yellow for possibly off-track, and green for on-track. Be proactive in providing business updates to your client. Share the status of key deliverables, specifically when you have roadblocks. Use your time wisely so your client can help you remove any obstacles, whether it's sending an email to someone or advising you how to take the next step. Come to the meeting with a prioritized list. Don't waste their time on things that can be sent in an email, like updates. Use your time for issues you can't easily resolve by email or require immediate attention.

In your first one-on-one, reestablish the foundational project details. Has anything changed since you scoped the work? Are the deliverables and timeline still accurate? Is your understanding of the client's priorities as it relates to your project still accurate, too? Now is also the time to ensure you have access to the network and any tools, documents, or portals.

Last, establish your clients' preferred communication method and style. Do they prefer email and informal communication, or would they like scheduled in-person meetings or video calls with a set agenda? Do they require any regular communication beyond the weekly one-on-one or should you simply schedule any additional touchpoints needed? Are there any other expectations, either cultural or business-related, that the client hasn't yet shared? Hash out any lingering details or unknowns to best set yourself up for success.

You need support from the entire team to deliver. It's critical that the clients introduce you to the broader team from the start to communicate who you are, what you are there to do, and why and how they're expected to help. You will not be set up for success if you come into a team that doesn't know why you are there or how your project contributes to the team's overall goals. They may try to sabotage you and impede your success. You need to know the key players on the team and proactively establish introductory meetings with each person individually to build a relationship. You also need access to key documents and shares to access material that will help you achieve your goals. Have these conversations and build a partnership with your client from the start to accelerate your success. Without the support of your clients and their team, it will be very difficult for you to succeed.

Sydney, a marketing and communications consultant, has perfected the team introduction. She coaches her client on the right way to introduce her to the broader team, which includes why Sydney is there and making it known that her goal is to help the team be successful and how they can raise their hands to get her support.

"I've literally created a 'How to work with Sydney' slide," she told me with a laugh. The slide includes things like how to contact her and her areas of subject-matter expertise, along with the information she needs when working with them on an ask, such as the outcomes, deadline, and so on. "I keep it very simple. It's really helpful for people to refer back to," Sydney added. "It also helps them know the right kind of work to even ask for because, while I am happy to help with anything, I want to make sure that they get the most value so I try to set the right expectations."

Great work setting yourself up for success! You have established clear expectations about how you will work with your client and how you will measure success metrics. Now, you are ready to deliver excellence every day. In the next chapter, we will build on your strong start to effectively manage your client and the work to achieve the desired outcome. It's time to showcase your expertise and spin that flywheel.

Reflection Questions

- Are the project deliverables clear to you? To the client?
- Have you set effective expectations with the client?
- Do you have a clear idea of how to deliver success for this contract?

EIGHT

DELIVER EXCELLENCE

"You can have everything in life you want,
if you will just help other people get what they want."
—ZIG ZIGLAR

S
YDNEY HAD ALWAYS DELIVERED EXCELLENCE.
In her corporate role as a marketing expert at a global tech
company, she consistently exceeded performance expectations and had a boss who was thrilled with her work. And yet, it
wasn't enough.

One afternoon, Sydney overheard her normally calm and good-
natured manager yelling into the phone from across the hall. When
her manager stormed into Sydney's office to ask if she could be there
for an 8:00 a.m. meeting the next day, Sydney knew what was next.
She'd seen enough of her colleagues get laid off, and it always began
with that sudden meeting request from your boss. Despite instinc-
tively knowing what that meeting would bring, Sydney was shocked.

"How could this happen to me?" she wondered. After eight years of outstanding work, she thought her job was secure.

Sure enough, at 8:00 a.m. the next day, Sydney was laid off along with roughly a third of her team. It had nothing to do with her performance. Someone at the top had simply decided that her group wasn't needed anymore. Her excellence hadn't been enough, and she never saw it coming.

That same day, Sydney was already on the hunt. She emailed her network with the news and asked them to send any leads or opportunities her way. She expected to find another role at the same company and get back to work. As the sole breadwinner of her household, not working was not an option. So, when a former colleague reached out to Sydney with a monthlong contract, she accepted. Consulting wasn't her long-term goal, but it would pay the bills while she kept looking for a more reliable job.

One month turned into two and then six and twelve. By the end of the first year, Sydney began to see that consulting was a viable profession. Ten years later and counting, Sydney is the epitome of a great consultant. She's had a steady pipeline of full-time work ever since that first project. She's made a name for herself, and she's made a good living.

As a full-time employee, delivering excellence wasn't enough. Now, as a consultant, it's everything. Sydney blends a mastery of her subject-matter expertise in messaging and communications with the distinctive way she shows up for her clients and their teams. She told me that clients make it clear to her, "We're hiring *you* and your skills. And if you're not available, help us find another Sydney."

What another Sydney looks like is someone who sets expectations and boundaries. Someone who can prioritize and self-regulate her workload. Someone who can do virtually anything—no job is too small, no challenge too big—provided it furthers the team's business goals. Someone who has fun and builds rapport while tapping into her expertise to enhance the team.

Sydney said something that I asked her to repeat: "If you treat the client who hires you as the only client, you develop a huge viral network." Meaning the client's success is her success, and anyone is a potential client. Her true motivation is to do great work and help her clients succeed. In doing so, she builds her project pipeline. That is delivery excellence.

When I first started consulting, I noticed inconsistencies in how consultants managed their projects. Clients seemed to have a hard time discerning which consultants added value. I got curious. How could I ensure that I was being the best possible resource for my clients? So, I began to ask clients what they looked for in a great consultant.

The first thing out of many clients' mouths was "rock star." Of course! Who doesn't want a rock star? And who doesn't want to *be* a rock star? But what defines that? When I dug deeper, they consistently shared what I coined as the ABCs of great consultants: Attitude, Build Trust, and Communication. Rock-star consultants have a great attitude, build trust in every interaction, and know how to communicate in writing and verbally. Now more than ever, these so-called soft skills are the differentiator between good and great consultants. These behaviors can seem elusive and hard to define, but you know them when you see them. The great consultants I've observed possess these attributes. Not coincidentally, they also have a strong pipeline of contracts and happy clients who refer and hire them again and again.

Delivering excellence is about how you show up and do the work that results in a successful outcome. As I've said before, it is the key to building your flywheel, because great work speaks for itself. And behind great work is often a great consultant. Every project is an opportunity to build a strong portfolio that supports your personal brand, develops new relationships, and enables you to thrive.

Over the past fourteen years, I have been fortunate to support and coach thousands of successful, long-term consultants. They attract clients, deliver amazing work, and make it all look easy. The right work comes effortlessly to them. They are respected and valued for their work and deliver results on their terms. They all share a client-first mindset. You, too, can be a rock star. Here's how.

Rock Star Rules
Rule 1: Your Client's Success Is Your Success

Make your client look great every time. Viewing the client's success as your own doesn't mean that you shouldn't take pride in your work. You should! But it *does* mean that, at the end of the day, it doesn't matter what you think of your work—it only matters what your client thinks. This is a huge shift for long-time corporate professionals.

I learned this quickly as a newbie consultant. For one of my first projects, a client hired me to create and deliver a marketing plan. I spent three months crafting what I believed was very good work. I was proud of my plan, and I couldn't wait to see it implemented and witness the results it was certain to deliver. When I handed it off, however, the client thanked me and acknowledged the good work, before informing me that the business was pivoting. The plan I had so painstakingly created was no longer a priority. My heart sank. I took it personally! *How could they not value my work?*

Then, I realized that I had done my job as a consultant. I'd successfully met my client's definition of success: completing and delivering the marketing plan. I had done the work and, though the business's focus had changed, my client was happy with the results. I realized that I had to replace my employee mindset with a consultant mindset. As an employee, it may have been career-limiting if my plan wasn't accepted by my manager, but as a consultant, things were different. Rather than be unhappy with myself, I simply needed to shift my perspective, recognize that I'd successfully delivered the project, and move on to the next.

That feeling was liberating. I've seen many professionals wrestle with this mindset shift when they first transition to consulting. The root of the issue is that they remain too attached to their work. As a consultant, you must intentionally let go of that attachment. Your only job is to deliver the work for the client *as they define success*. You may have a different idea of what the business needs and, though you can choose to share your perspective, you can't take it personally when the client decides to go in another direction. You are there to help them be successful and offer your guidance, advice, expertise, support, or whatever it is that they need. Ultimately, it's not your job to make the business decisions—it's your client's.

A few years ago, one of our consultants, Mark, came to me in frustration when his client didn't act on his advice. He went on and on about how right he was and how wrong the client was. I encouraged him to pause, shift his perspective, and consider a few questions. *What if you don't have all the information? Are you letting your ego get the best of you? While unfortunate if they make a bad decision, is it possible that they don't see it that way?*

Mark realized that he had become too emotionally attached to the work. He needed the reminder that he had delivered on what the client hired him to do. Whether the client acted on the work he delivered was outside his control.

Remember that, as a consultant, your number one goal is to do great work, as seen by your client. If you think it's great work but your client does not, where does that get you beyond a burned bridge for a referral and possibly damaged reputation? Don't get me wrong. Your opinion and advice are often highly valuable to your client. However, when that guidance isn't taken, it's not personal.

Christopher, the business strategist who shared his networking lunch strategy, is widely regarded as a rock star. In his work, Christopher is always looking to create a "one plus one equals four" kind of scenario for his clients and, as a result, for himself.

"A big organization is charged politically," he said to me. "If you're not helping your client get ahead and navigate that landscape, they're going to get eaten, and as a result, I get eaten, too. So, it's in my best interest to ensure that they're shining. That's why I try to take extraordinary steps."

Rule 2: Proactively Manage Expectations

As a consultant, a contract extension or client referral are the ultimate compliments. They are the goal of every consultant with every project. To achieve that goal, you must set clear expectations at the start and deliver value every day.

We reviewed expectation setting in detail in Chapter 7. Set yourself up for success with well-defined project scope, logistics, invoicing, communication cadence, and more. It is your responsibility to be proactive and then hold to those commitments. If you notice that the work you are doing doesn't seem to align with your client's priorities, it's a great opportunity to have a conversation and recommend how your time and energy could sync with his or her priorities.

Whether you realize it or not, you are being reviewed every day. Even though consulting offers the ultimate flexibility, people notice how you show up and the quality of your work. When you join a video call, do you look professional or like you just rolled out of bed? When you speak, are you prepared or distracted? A successful consultant has self-imposed structure and learns quickly about the value of time-blocking to achieve results. Every moment you have with your client matters. You will either show up as having done the work or not—you can't fake impact. That is why consulting is so attractive to results-oriented people. It's all about outcomes. You are on the hook for knowing what needs to be done and making it happen.

I remember the end of one of my first contracts. My client was so impressed with what I had delivered. It had seemed easy to me—I was hired to deliver on one project, in an area that I had expertise in, with no distractions. That ability to focus on my craft showed me the power of contract work. You can deliver amazing results because that is all you are hired to do. It increases your success rate, boosts your confidence, and continues to build your brand.

Rule 3: Add Value Every Day

Great consultants have a high EQ (emotional intelligence). They successfully blend hard and soft skills to demonstrate competence and character and add value. Have you ever worked with someone who was good at his or her craft, but had a low emotional intelligence that was difficult to work with? Managers rarely want to hire people they don't like, even if those people are really good at what they do.

Deanna, the training and development expert, credits her ability to extend contracts to curiosity, an important soft skill. Her contract for an ecommerce client recently ballooned from three months to two years. She believes that the best consultants are curious, observant, invested, and interested in their clients' organizations, taking the time to spot gaps and note areas for improvement. In doing so, Deanna identifies needs her client didn't even realize existed and sets herself up to potentially extend the length and scope of her contracts.

"Being a consultant lends itself nicely to those things, because as an outside observer with a focused workload, you have the headspace and fresh perspective that those within the organization don't," she shared with me.

Beyond delivering great work, which is a given, the most in-demand consultants are keenly attuned to knowing what their clients need and adding value every day.

Rule 4: Earn Trust to Build Relationships

You build the relationship with your client one conversation at a time. Every interaction is an opportunity to show up, listen, deliver on your promises, and earn the client's trust.

"Trust is built in drops and lost in buckets," said Kevin Plank, the CEO of Under Armour. I like this visual. Think about every interaction as a drop. Over time you are either building trust and credibility or losing it. Trust is built every day in the micro moments. Are you doing what you say? Are you showing up when you say you will? Are you engaged in the work?

I've had clients say to me over the years: "I'm not seeing my consultant online today. I don't think they're doing the work." Usually, this isn't about the consultant being online, it's that the consultant is not delivering value. This is a conversation about the expected work to be done. Therefore, a detailed statement of work with clear deliverables is critical because you can refer to it and objectively assess if the work is on track. And if it is not on track, then it's a conversation about expected work hours and availability. Did priorities change? Is there a roadblock that the consultant cannot overcome and needs the client to help with? Or something else entirely?

Also, be aware of your visibility. If senior leadership doesn't know what you are doing, your project could get cut around budget time. You need to be sure the budget owners are aware of the work you are doing and, more important, how it impacts the business. If the key decision makers have no view of your work, and your client lacks the right level of influence, you may get lost in the shuffle. Help your clients help you by being an advocate for them and preparing your work so that they can share it with their leadership. Clients won't always represent your work exactly as you might want them to and you won't always have the opportunity to be in the room with leadership, but don't let that deter you. Give your clients what they need to present and share your work with leadership. It's obviously best if you can get in front of the decision makers to present, as you are closest to it, but there may be politics at play. All you can do is set your clients up for success to credibly share your work. If you make your clients look great, then you look great, so you have the same goal.

Relationship building is key to being a successful rock-star consultant. Make time to connect with your client and the team. Get to know them personally. After all, we are hardwired for personal connection. You need it as much as your client does.

Rule 5: Manage Your Personal Brand

Stay above the fray of any workplace interpersonal issues and say no to drama. It does not serve you to take sides with anyone on the team.

Think of yourself as Switzerland. You are a neutral party. It's your job to add value and complete your deliverables, not to get caught up in unproductive team dynamics.

Your reputation precedes you as a consultant, so regularly monitor how others perceive you. As Jeff Bezos famously said: "Your brand is what others say about you when you are not in the room." Make sure that you are living your brand and showing up every day intentionally demonstrating your authentic words. If you need a refresher, go back to Chapter 3 and review the personal brand questions to see your authentic words in action. Always play to your strengths.

Rule 6: Support, Don't Compete with Your Client

I once worked for a very driven client, and I was excited to work with her. But very shortly into the project I sensed her resistance. It seemed like she didn't trust me, but I wasn't sure why.

I quickly realized that she felt like we were in competition, maybe that I even wanted her job. So, I decided to address this with her because I needed her support to be successful. I reminded her that I intentionally took myself off the traditional career path. I was no longer competing with her for advancement, and my sole job was to make her look great so *she* could get promoted, not me. Her face softened. Just hearing those words helped her see that I was on her side.

Heidi, the business strategist who starts each project with intention, shared her experience directly addressing any client fears or insecurities head on. "I tell them: 'I have chosen to be a consultant. I am not interested in your role. My job is to make you and your team look good. What can I do to help do that?'"

You may run into this, too. Occasionally, clients will feel threatened by your work. But it usually isn't about you, it's about their own insecurities, and who can blame them? Working in corporate America can be cutthroat. People are competing for their share of the annual bonus and stock, title, and advancement opportunities. It's human nature to want to stand out and be chosen.

Be confident in who you are as a consultant and the value you can offer your clients. Don't dance around the issue. Remind your clients why you are there and that your intention is to help them succeed. Look for every opportunity, big or small, to practice empathy and build trust.

Rule 7: Adapt to Your Client's Needs

Being agile and adaptable to your client's needs is a powerful skill. Rock-star consultants are aware of how to show up for their clients in each moment by reading their body language, energy, and the environment. You may have your agenda for the day, but if your clients have been thrown a curve ball, you need to pause, listen, and change your approach to meet your clients where they need you at that moment. These little things make a huge difference in how you achieve results. Harness your superpowers and understand the role you need to play for your clients at any given time.

Let's review the five most common roles.

1. COACH: Listen, understand, and guide
   - Listen and ask questions
   - Be a strategy sounding board and mirror in client conversations
   - Help the client come to the right answer

2. ADVISOR: Leverage your expertise to teach and do the work

- Help your client connect the dots between work and outcomes when necessary
- Ensure priorities line up
- Demonstrate competence, confidence, and knowledge
- Strive to be friendly, adaptable, and appreciative in all interactions

3. INFLUENCER: Bring disparate groups together by understanding individual motivations

- Demonstrate strong cross-group collaboration skills
- Be approachable and open-minded
- Represent your clients with maturity
- Help execute productive dialogs
- Consider the consequences of actions
- Encourage all points of view and succinctly summarize them for decision making

4. DO-ER: Get things done, make it happen

- Do what you say, always
- Over deliver and under commit
- Maintain 100 percent client focus
- Stay curious on ways to make a bigger impact
- Demonstrate enthusiasm for the work—eager and energetic
- Desire to make a difference every day
- Get clear on objectives
- Be flexible, able to adjust without losing sight of objectives

5. PROBLEM SOLVER: Always look for ways to help your clients overcome their problems, not contribute to them

- Uncover issues, recommend solutions, and knock down obstacles
- Create order out of chaos
- Remain analytical and objective
- Offer new ideas and approaches
- Be proactive
- See potential landmines while offering ways to navigate or mitigate them

Rule 8: Set Clear Boundaries

Heidi shared the example of how to handle a project that's become too time-consuming. She gives it a week or so, and if it gets to be too much, she tells her client: "My workload is heavy right now. If this is short-term, that's okay. If not, is there someone I can hand this off to, or can you help me prioritize?"

"They have no way of knowing unless I tell them," she said.

Revisit your earlier expectation-setting exercise often to make sure you are working when you said you would work, and fulfill the expectations of the contract. If you find yourself working more than your original commitment, it's time to hit the reset button and talk with your client. As Heidi notes, it's likely that the client has no idea. Often other team members may give you work that isn't part of your job and, in an effort to be a great consultant, you keep saying yes. While this is well intentioned, it is the fastest path to burnout and can damage your credibility.

Part of being a rock-star consultant is knowing how to reign in scope creep.

Take Amelia, a social media consultant. She was a pleaser. She did whatever her client wanted. After a few months on a project, Amelia found herself stressed out, working around the clock, and always on call. It wasn't what she signed up for. "How did this contract go sideways so quickly?" she wondered. She reviewed her original statement of work and discovered that she was doing a lot of work beyond the project scope.

Amelia went to her client with a professional and helpful tone and shared with her a list of the additional work she was doing outside what was scoped. She also made a recommendation for the work she believed she should be focusing on and the other tasks that she didn't have time to complete, based on her experience. The client had been unaware of the added tasks and agreed with her recommendation.

By taking the time to educate the client on scope creep, Amelia could focus on the priorities for the business and maintain her boundaries. Alternatively, she could have suggested that the work out-of-scope either be reassigned to someone else on the team or re-evaluated by the client to determine its current priority.

I have observed that clients often are unaware of scope expansion until the consultant proactively brings it to their attention. Therefore, it's critical to do a thorough expectation setting and scope definition up front. It becomes the basis for your work. Sometimes project goals change and that is perfectly reasonable. If the work has shifted, have a conversation with your client. What are the new goals? What does success look like? And are you still the right person for the work? Always make sure that you are placing yourself on a successful path to achieve the deliverable.

This is a hard one for those of us who care about work immensely and give freely without setting boundaries. However, over time, exhaustion builds to the point of frustration. I have talked many consultants off the ledge when they have burned the candle at both ends to deliver beyond the scope of work. Usually by that point, they focus on the money and demand more, but it isn't about the money. It's about learning to set boundaries and respecting your expertise. It's about intentionally delivering the work to your client as it was scoped from the beginning. Therefore, taking the time up front to clearly set expectations is an important factor in your success.

If you are someone who goes above and beyond at any hour of the day, I'm talking to you. If you work that way as a consultant, you will become frustrated or burned out or both. Most people choose consulting because it gives them more control over their schedule and their choice of work. If, like so many of us, you have been conditioned to work all the time, always reacting, then consulting requires approaching work in a new way. Be relentless in your pursuit of clear scope, proactive communication, and strong boundaries, even when it requires difficult conversations that push you beyond your comfort zone.

Rule 9: Ask for Feedback

Feedback is a gift. So, ask for it. While it doesn't always feel great in the moment to receive feedback, accept it as an opportunity for growth so it can serve you well. Some clients may be uncomfortable sharing feedback with you; others will be open to it. I would much rather know what I'm doing well and where I need to improve than not knowing the client's opinion.

Once I received feedback from a manager that I was indecisive. At first, I was hurt and angry because I consider myself to be an action-oriented person. However, it provided me an opportunity to reflect. I realized that I would be remiss if I didn't try to understand why this manager had that perception of me and seek to understand his point of view. We all have blind spots. So, I asked him why he thought I was indecisive. It turns out that at times I could be too collaborative which he perceived as indecisive. I have always considered myself a collaborative person and I realized that if I weighed too many opinions for too long that it could result in delayed decisions. I appreciated him sharing his point of view and his perspective increased my awareness of how I make decisions. Now when I catch myself delaying making decisions, I pause and recognize it's usually because I'm weighing too many viewpoints. When that happens I remember the feedback, and move to decisiveness, even when it feels a little uncomfortable.

Use your weekly client check-in meetings wisely. To solicit constructive feedback, ask these two questions on a regular basis:

What do you value that I am doing? What more can I do?

These open-ended questions allow your client to highlight what they view as important, so you know to keep doing those activities. Also, they may share areas to focus on more, so you know where to shift your energy and where their priorities lie. Staying ahead of your client is not easy but this is the difference between good and great consultants. Asking these questions often helps you and your client stay aligned.

Rule 10: End on a High Note

Before you start asking for referrals and references, you need to successfully close out your contract, tie up any loose ends, and leave things better than when you arrived. This step is critical to managing your reputation, because if you leave people hanging and poor documentation is your final impression then it will be difficult to secure a positive referral for your next contract.

How you start is how you finish, remember? Now that you are at the end of your contract, continue to deliver value and conclude the project with positivity and professionalism. Be consistent in your delivery to ensure client success and create raving fans. Follow these vetted best practices:

- **Create a transition document:** Include everything that you delivered in a single document and post to a CloudShare for you and your client. Make it easy for them to understand the status of the work and any open items.
- **Leave the team better:** When you end your contract, you should be able to definitively articulate how your work and contributions made the team better.
- **Your success is directly connected to your client's success:** How did you improve your client's profile? Did you do work that will help them stand out in their next review?

Last, but not least, Heidi finishes each project strong. "Don't overlook the hand off," she advised. She always provides the client with a thorough hand-off document, something that includes all the projects she's worked on with links to key documents and contacts, as well as recommendations and next steps. "Everything in one place," she told me. "So, they can open a single document and find everything that they need."

Do You Feel Like a Rock Star Yet?

You have successfully navigated and managed the delivery of your stated deliverables. You have shown up with a client-first mindset, added value in every conversation, created and cultivated new relationships, and grown your portfolio. You are living the consultant life.

Now that your flywheel is in motion, you are undoubtedly thinking about what's next. Have the seeds you planted for new opportunities sprouted? Do you want to jump into a new contract or take a break? Whatever you choose, now is the time to reflect and refresh. Rejuvenate your mind, body, and spirit. Don't skip this step. It helps to center you, keep you on your desired path, and fill up your tank so that you can continue sharing your gifts with the world.

Reflection Questions

- How are you adding value to your client every day?
- Are you checking in weekly and proactively sharing your status?
- Can you articulate your results and how you have made the team better?

NINE

REFLECT AND REFRESH

*"We must never become too busy sawing
to take time to sharpen the saw."*
—STEPHEN COVEY[1]

A S A CONSULTANT, YOU INVEST considerable time focusing on your client. Now, it's time to focus on yourself.

Keri, the startup marketing strategist, views life as a marathon, not a sprint. Maintaining that forward momentum takes self-discipline and stamina. It also demands intention. There aren't any performance reviews, company retreats, or leadership huddles on the company's strategic direction in contract work. So, Keri created her own. A few years into her career as an independent consultant, she built an annual review and reset process for one.

At the end of each year, after she wraps up her books, Keri takes a day to reflect. If she's feeling especially motivated, she may even build a short PowerPoint presentation to present to herself. She looks at things like how many clients she had, how much money she made, and how much time she was able to take off. She compiles client wins such as Client A got that funding round and other proof points including Client B improved its ROI by 25 percent after executing the strategic plan she created. She identifies her favorite and least-favorite projects and reflects on why they landed on those respective lists. Was it the people she worked with? Was it the client's engagement? Was it the type of strategy work or the impact she made? Whatever the answers, positive or negative, Keri identifies actionable ways to adjust her process and intentionally attract and land more work that feeds her soul.

Those annual reviews have made Keri a better consultant. They've helped her fine-tune how she sells, scopes, and delivers projects. They've also given her the clarity to focus on the kind of work she loves and shift her ideal client from enterprise organizations with local headquarters to funded startups in growth mode.

And Keri doesn't just reflect at the end of the year. She builds brief, but impactful review time at the end of each project. She solicits direct client feedback with a survey once each project is complete. She asks targeted questions to uncover which of her standard deliverables had the most value, if she's following through on her core promise, in which areas she exceeded expectations, and where there's room for improvement. Those surveys provide her with valuable information to improve her delivery excellence and an opportunity to capture client testimonials.

In this way, Keri is intentional about driving her consulting business forward by pursuing the work she loves while continuously improving how she delivers impact. She also builds a balanced routine for herself, so she can recharge and prioritize herself as a habit and not just when her projects end.

"I have workaholic tendencies, so unless I schedule my personal priorities first, all the things that are important to me and help me refresh tend to get pushed out," Keri said. A planner to the core, Keri starts each week by creating a color-coded calendar, and literally puts herself first. She blocks out time for the things that nourish her, "working out, getting together with friends, date nights with my husband, fun activities with my kids," before scheduling blocks of time for meetings and focused project work.

Keri is mindful of how she spends her time and the trajectory of the career path she's built for herself. Approach your consultant journey with the same intention. Carve out time to routinely pause, reflect, and refresh. As Stephen Covey puts it, leave room to "sharpen the saw."

In Covey's *7 Habits of Highly Effective People*, he outlines how to preserve and enhance your greatest asset: You. He offers advice for caring for your body, mind, heart, and spirit, all in the pursuit of making reflection and self-care a regular habit. In this chapter, I'll share how to reflect and refresh and why it's critical to your success as a consultant. My goal? Your success, happiness, and well-being. After all, you are worth it!

Reflect

Let's make reflection a habit. When your contract ends, it's easy to jump headlong into the next opportunity. Instead, pause. Use this time with intention. Hit the brakes, reflect on the project, and refresh your body, mind, and spirit. Successful consultants have built the discipline to regularly remind themselves of what they love, celebrate their accomplishments, and plan for what's next.

As we saw with Keri's story, she regroups after each project, and then stiches those reflections together in her annual review for one. Some consultants reflect after each project; others quarterly or annually. The structure and frequency are secondary. What's important is that it works for you. Choose the cadence that fits your style and hold yourself accountable for following through.

Stop to reflect and ask yourself:

- What were the project highlights? The lowlights?
- What elements of the work do you want to do more of? Less of?
- What type of work are you excited about and feeling drawn toward?
- What skills do you want to develop? How will you approach learning (e.g., find a mentor, take an online class, or read a book)?
- What could you have done differently to make the project more successful?
- What did you learn from how you managed your relationship with the client?
- What outcomes did you achieve for the client?
- When you add this project to your résumé and profile, what are the most impactful elements to highlight?

You could also take a page from Keri's book and request feedback from your client, whether it's a formal survey or a casual follow-up email or conversation. Keep it brief, and focus on gathering specific, constructive feedback to help you refine your craft.

Now is also the moment to ask your clients to help you. Ask while your work and impact are still fresh in the clients' mind. After every project, ask your clients to provide you with a testimonial, ideally in the form of a LinkedIn recommendation. Make it easy for them. Draft a proposed recommendation, highlighting the key areas where you added value that align with your personal brand and including quantifiable outcomes whenever possible. Once clients agree to provide a testimonial, offer your draft as a starting point. Most clients appreciate when you do the heavy lifting, and they will edit anything they don't agree with. Taking that initiative will increase your chances of getting it done and ensuring that it says what you want about you and your work.

Also, let your clients know how they can help you land your next contract. Ask if they know of anyone who needs project support or someone who could benefit from your skill set. If nothing else, inquire if they can introduce you to someone in their network who could help to open doors, grow your skills, or expand your perspective. Plant those seeds.

Sometimes a project isn't successful. It happens to all of us. We take on a contract and think we can succeed. At some point, we realize that either the work wasn't what we anticipated, or we try to deliver and it doesn't land as we intended. Life happens. I love this reminder from Arianna Huffington: "Failure is not the opposite of success, it's part of success."[2] We all fail at times. Maybe the deliverable didn't get met, whether it was within your control or not. Maybe you could have built a stronger relationship with your client and the team. Maybe the scope creeped so significantly that you were unable to rein it in. No matter the reason, if you find yourself in this situation, treat it as a teachable moment. What happened? What can you do differently next time? What did you learn about yourself or your skills? And, if the client was kind enough to share some constructive feedback, how can you use that information to your benefit in future projects?

Shift your perspective from failure to learning. Adopt a growth mindset. We are always learning. We are never done. It's not just you, we are all a work in progress. Nurture your self-awareness and move forward with confidence and optimism. In Chapter 6, I stressed that a positive, resilient mindset is the key to finding a great contract. The same is true now. Reflect after each project to continuously improve your craft and deliver the results that will keep your flywheel spinning.

Refresh Your Personal Brand

Revisit the foundation that you built in Part II. Does your personal brand still ring true? Are your authentic words still how you want others to describe you? Does your personal brand statement accurately reflect the work you love to do and what you want to be known for? Walk back through the five steps to build your personal brand. Most likely, many of your answers will remain unchanged, and you can rework specific elements as needed to refresh your words, statement, and success stories. Pursue the work that lights you up, and that work may change as your life does.

Don't just reflect. Write it down! Capture your accomplishments and the results you delivered. The more detail and quantitative proof points you use to describe your outcomes, the better. These data points and success metrics are the evidence you need to build a strong foundation for your personal brand. Tell your story consistently, everywhere. Update your LinkedIn profile and your résumé. Add your latest project details, again emphasizing outcomes and results. Feature testimonials from your client and any teammates or stakeholders that worked closely with you. Ensure that your story effectively positions you to attract your ideal work and client.

Now that you have refreshed your personal brand, let's shift to refresh your body and mind.

Refresh Your Body and Mind

My body was talking to me, but it took a few months for me to listen. The dizziness and exhaustion came in waves. Some days I would sit down or grab nearby furniture to steady myself. Other days I struggled to overcome bouts of heavy fatigue. But each time the waves receded, I pushed them to the back of my mind and kept going at the only pace I knew, full-steam ahead.

One day in a meeting in my company's conference room the whole room began to spin. I could see the person talking, but I did not comprehend what she was saying. Nauseated and disoriented, I couldn't see straight. The wave wasn't receding as it usually did. This time I wasn't able to just push through it. I excused myself and made my way to the restroom where I sat on the tile floor waiting for the wave to pass. It was almost an hour before I could stand up. My colleague, Tami, came to check on me and was worried when she saw me on the floor. I was embarrassed. She helped me get a ride home. I went straight to bed. My body clearly needed sleep. The next day, I got up and jumped back into my normal routine as if nothing had happened. Looking back, that day should have been enough of a wake-up call for me to listen to my body. But in the moment, it wasn't. I plunged back into my busy life with all its seemingly important priorities and responsibilities. It took passing out on my bathroom floor a year later for me to finally stop and listen.

It was 9:00 a.m. on a Thursday, thirty minutes before a business call that I was not looking forward to. I was getting ready at home before I made the short walk to the office. All I remember was feeling the sudden need to vomit and leaning quickly over the toilet. I woke up—minutes? seconds? later—flat on my back. My husband was at work, my oldest son was at school, my youngest son was still sleeping peacefully, and the house was quiet.

I opened my eyes hesitantly, blinking as I looked around. *What happened? Why was I laying on the bathroom floor?* I didn't know how long I had been there. I couldn't move my arms and legs. It felt like a dream where my appendages each weighed a hundred pounds, and I was superglued to the floor. I'd never felt anything like it before. After several minutes and some grunting, I came unglued.

I slowly crawled into the adjoining guest bedroom and lay there on my guest bed. I stared at the ceiling. *What was happening to me? Was I sick? What should I do?* By then, I'd missed the meeting. I felt frustrated and guilty realizing I had been taking my health for granted.

I called my husband and told him what happened. Concerned, he immediately came home to drive me to the doctor. They ran a battery of tests and found nothing. My heart was healthy, the doctor told me, maybe it was stress? I didn't find that advice very helpful. What am I supposed to do about that? I didn't see how I could change my life-style in that moment, but I clearly needed to do something. This had to be the last warning sign.

Don't wait until you're sprawled out on the bathroom floor. Listen to your body. It speaks in whispers at first, but if you don't listen, it will whack you upside the head. I was lucky. I was unhurt, no blood or broken bones. But my body was clearly trying to tell me something. I recall hearing Arianna Huffington speak at a conference about her moment of truth when she collapsed, hitting her desk and breaking her jaw. That moment changed her life. It propelled her to start Thrive and speak out on the importance of sleep after years of exhaustion and sleep deprivation. I relate to her story as an accomplished businesswoman juggling endless priorities.

After a lot of reflection, I came to this conclusion. Over the years, as I built my business and raised my boys, the stress gradually accumulated. I had allowed myself to take on an inordinate amount of personal and professional stress, and I didn't have anyone to blame but myself. I didn't ask for help. I didn't know how to. I placed caring for everyone else, including their emotional stress, before caring for myself. I was a pleaser, and I didn't understand the concept of boundaries. I was incapable of saying no. Plus, I got caught up in the excitement of building a business. It is fun and exciting to be a successful entrepreneur. It felt like a drug and was highly addicting. I fell into the dangerous trap of letting the priorities of others become more important than my own. It wasn't sustainable, and my body had finally had enough.

I made a commitment to add regular self-care to my routine. I began a daily meditation practice with the Headspace app. It has been amazing to witness how just ten minutes of meditation can calm my brain. I attended a few yoga retreats with friends, which filled my spirit immensely. There's nothing like a good yoga class with friends. I got a dog, a Cavalier King Charles Spaniel named Winston, who forces me to get outside in the fresh air for our daily walks. I experience joy every time I pet him. I jokingly call him my emotional support dog, which really isn't a joke because he has become our team mascot and provides love to everyone.

I also decided to surrender. For me, that means focusing on being present and appreciating the moment rather than doing, doing, doing. I am a work in progress and some days are better than others. Sometimes I feel guilty taking time for myself, but I try to think about it as a necessary way to keep me operating at 100 percent. I am working on asking for help. That's a hard one for me. I have a very supportive husband and two teenage boys and an amazing team at Simplicity Consulting. As every business owner knows, it's all about the team, and I am grateful and proud of them for continuing to advance their own development.

Keri's observation at the top of the chapter checks out—working as a consultant is like running a marathon. You must pace yourself and adapt to the changing environment. Build in routine breaks to recharge and sustain yourself. But each contract is also like a sprint. You run hard for a limited period of time and then rest and recover so that you can sprint again. In both scenarios, you must carve out time for rest and recovery to be at your peak performance. It could be one day a quarter or a year, whatever works best for you, just do it. If you feel like it's too self-indulgent and you don't have the time, then you especially need to do it. I see you. I was the same way.

It's also important to practice self-care in small, daily habits that aren't glamorous but necessary. "Good self-care is typically more difficult and less glamorous than treating yourself," Emily Bilek, a clinical assistant professor at the University of Michigan's Depression Center told HuffPost. "It means doing things like having good sleep hygiene, getting a little more exercise, staying hydrated, taking medication as prescribed, eating at regular intervals, creating healthy boundaries, and taking a break from social media." Self-care is hard work, she says. It isn't glamorous or flashy, but the payoff is rewarding.[3]

Self-care may look different for everyone. Find those small moments in your day that bring you joy and rejuvenation. Self-care is a journey, not a destination. And on that journey, it's best to follow the advice of the airline experts: Put your own mask on first before helping anyone else.

Design Your Life

One of my favorite books to recommend is *Designing Your Life* by Bill Burnett and Dave Evans. It's a practical and detailed approach for anyone looking to create a joy-filled life. Burnett includes an exercise to explore the many alternate lives you could imagine for yourself. The point is to recognize that there is no one set path or idea for your life. There are many lives you could live happily and productively. You get to choose. Use your personal brand to set your course. Decide on the path you want to pursue and set yourself up with daily habits to stay on course and reinforce your direction.

"It's your life by design," said Krissi, a creative marketing consultant I've worked with since the early days of Simplicity Consulting. Krissi wholeheartedly believes in the benefit of daily habits. She has the same routine each morning.

She wakes up at 5:00 a.m., makes her bed, and puts on her workout clothes to ensure that she fits exercise into her daily schedule. After making a double espresso, she sits down with her notebook to begin her very own "G3 Method": Gratitude + Goals + Grinds (as in coffee grinds). As she journals, Krissi asks herself:

- Gratitude: What am I grateful for in this moment?
- Affirmation: Who am I today and what do I want the world to know about me?
- Positivity: Where's my positivity coming from and how do I chase it? What struggle or challenge am I dealing with and how will I lead with positivity and optimism to overcome it?
- Motivation: How do I mine my motivation? What is the thing that I am holding back on or procrastinating about? How do I find the internal motivation to get after it?

- Courage: Where is the courage within myself? How will I
  step into fear that might be holding me back, but lean into
  it knowing that I will get better because of it?

Everything she does, she does with a smile. "My disposition and my attitude have always been the things that have my clients bringing me back," she said.

Krissi's daily routine fuels her infectious energy. It offers the right mix of inspiration, meditation, and organization to set her up for success. When she wraps up her morning G3, Krissi writes out her schedule for the day. She keeps the notebook open on her desk throughout the day to keep her on track.

"It's a quick way for me to see what I have going on and to be honest about what is viable to achieve in the day," Krissi said. "I find it very helpful to write it down first so I can see where the time sucks are, adjust, and ultimately set myself up for daily success."

Krissi and Keri aren't the only ones who use their schedules to hold themselves accountable. Many of the consultants you met in this book schedule time for sanity breaks and self-care.

Heidi, the business strategist who starts each project with intention, schedules her day with her needs in mind. She starts each morning with a workout and puts it on her calendar, so she doesn't end up letting work take priority over her health. She eats dinner with her husband and three children.

"If I need to get back on the computer in the evening, I do," she told me over email. "But this way I stop work at a reasonable hour and have time with my family and give them my attention."

When Heidi starts to feel overwhelmed, she hits the refresh button by writing a prioritized list of work items. She starts by tackling the most critical items, and—this "and" is important!—she does something to recharge, such as taking a glass of wine into a hot bath or curling up with a good book before bed or sipping whiskey with her husband. She's conscious of reducing her stress levels by pairing an urgent action item with a nonwork activity that fills her cup.

Similar to Keri's color-coded calendaring, Sydney puts everything from work to fun in her calendar. The marketing and communications consultant takes stock at the start of the week to assess the plan, and then again at the end of the week to determine the reality. This plan versus actual view helps her to see how her time was spent and which areas she can improve in the future.

"When my days are well planned," she said in an email, "I feel no guilt for taking time out during the workday to get lunch, run an errand, exercise, or walk my dogs."

Catharine, the storyteller with a strong personal brand, has created a daily routine to build her mental and physical strength.

"I started driving out every morning to a peaceful, open country trail that allows no bikes, just walkers and dogs, with my dog," she shared in an email. "It gives me a routine and makes me think I'm getting somewhere, while helping me focus, build strength, and reduce anxiety."

Catharine's routine doesn't just benefit her mental state, it benefits her work, too. She gets a lot of writing ideas while walking. Both she and her dog are hooked: "Tomorrow marks seventy-five walks in a row. I mark the numbers on my mirror so I can see my progress. My dog now stares me down daily with his intrepid spirit of 'Hey, are we going?'"

Invest in Yourself

A few years into her consulting career, Sydney had a startling realization.

Nobody is looking out for my professional development, she thought. I have to go seek it out myself, and I probably have to pay for it.

It's important to Sydney that she continuously challenge herself to learn and grow, and maybe it's important to you, too. She takes on projects that have an element of newness and challenge, whether it's a new-to-her product or team or a different twist on her core deliverables. Sydney routinely asks herself: Is this work what I want to be known for? Where am I going long-term, and where is this work getting me? Her intrinsic desire for growth also pushed her to register for a nine-month accredited coaching program. Though it wasn't cheap, she wanted to have another skill set and avenue for income. In her contract work, she uses language learned in the program to dialogue with clients and informally coach herself.

We've already touched on the importance of a growth mindset. Embracing lifelong learning requires an investment in yourself. It's how you invest your time, reading books and articles and DIYing new skills, and how you invest your money, from professional development courses and certifications to wellness and health expenses.

Cassondra, the senior business program manager with her A and B lists, keeps constant tabs on what skills are in demand and what new products and technologies are trending. "I'm always looking outside my skill set to see what other needs exist," she said. Years ago, when she worried about the renewal status of her current project, she heard that SharePoint was hot. She immediately went out and signed up for a class so she could learn and use those skills in her next project. Today, it's Microsoft Azure. She's educated herself on the cloud solution, so she has the language to be knowledgeable about it in her project work. There will always be that next thing to learn, and Cassondra is dedicated to playing the long game.

Congratulations! You are living the lifestyle many dream about but you had the courage to take the action steps and make it a reality. I hope you have realized that you have everything you need to create the life you want on your terms. My goal is to empower you to realize your greatness. Just as Glinda the Good Witch from *The Wizard of Oz* says, "You've always had the power my dear, you just had to learn it for yourself."

Go forth and be awesome. Land the work you love and create the life you want.

Reflection Questions

- What accomplishment are you most proud of?
- What activity most refreshes you?
- What do you want to do next?

CONCLUSION

You did it!

You have done the work. You have built the foundation and set your flywheel in motion to create the life you want and take control of your destiny. And you have proven that you have everything you need to make it happen. I am so proud of you.

You are the CEO of your career. Work and life by your design. How does it feel to be living and working on your terms? It takes courage and perseverance to forge your own path. You likely confronted some self-doubt and wavering confidence. But you persisted. You had some of your own big and small lightbulb moments that emboldened your ability to articulate and go after what you want. You took the initiative to do the work you love, however you love to do it.

I wrote this book to show you an alternative career path and equip you to thrive in the new world of work. Remember that you always have a choice. In life, we can choose fear or opportunity. You have chosen opportunity. You have taken charge of your life and created opportunity for yourself. Your work and life can be whatever you want it to be. The choice is yours. You have options. You always do even if you do not think you do.

Contract work is a viable alternative to traditional employment. You can work differently. You can have a successful consulting career. You are ready to handle what life throws your way because you have done your foundation and flywheel work which allows you to be agile and nimble with your career options. You have built your foundation which includes your personal brand, defining your ideal work, client and rate and your flywheel consists of landing contracts, delivering excellence, reflecting on what's next and refreshing your body, mind, and spirit. These core components are timeless. Use them as your touchstone. Refer to them when life undoubtedly changes as your north star. You have done a lot of work so stay true to yourself and keep this book handy. Check in on your answers to the reflection questions often to make sure you are on your intended course.

The ultimate benefits of consulting are freedom and flexibility. You earn them by taking consistent actions every day. Building authentic relationships with your client and colleagues demonstrates trust. Delivering excellence in your work and showing how you add value builds your personal brand and keeps your flywheel spinning. Continuing to invest in yourself and taking responsibility for your own growth and development sets you apart as a true professional dedicated to honing your craft. It's all about creating as many options as possible for yourself so that you can choose what's next as your work and life priorities may shift.

Work and life are always changing, just like you. Over time, your definition of success may change, too. That is the beauty of being the captain of your ship—you get to call the shots. As your work and life demands ebb and flow, you can keep your boat afloat and navigate the winds of change by adjusting your sails. There is no one-size-fits-all career path for anyone, and you have more options than ever before.

By taking control and choosing yourself, you are setting an example. Your journey will help to illuminate lightbulb moments in those around you. You will show the world that you have everything you need to make it happen, and you'll instill the promise of that hope and inspiration in others. You will quickly become the person others will seek out when they are going through their own career reinvention. Along the way, you can teach and guide others. Just as Maya Angelou said, "When you learn, teach, when you get, give."[1] Now that you have this knowledge, what else can you do with it? How can you help others who are struggling to find success at work? Pay it forward. It's your turn to help others successfully navigate their own path.

You have the power to improve the world with your unique talents and contributions. I hope this book has inspired and enabled you to step into your greatness. Do the thing that makes you come alive. Let your light shine. The world needs it, and so do you.

APPENDIX 1
FREQUENTLY ASKED QUESTIONS

Visit www.lisahufford.com for templates and worksheets that accompany this book.

Over the years I have received these common questions that you likely have, too. I hope this FAQ format helps you easily get the answers you need.

Q. My partner thinks consulting is too risky and wants me to take a full-time job. But I want the flexibility of doing contract work. How do I convince him/her?

A. Get curious with your partner. Ask questions about their concerns with you working on contracts. Once uncovered, you can address those concerns with a plan. For example, I've heard from many professionals over the years share that their spouse is concerned about potential inconsistent income. If that is the issue, then factor that into your overall pay rate. Also, plan to keep a minimum amount of money in a separate account as your rainy-day fund with at least six months of expenses. This is a good financial wellness practice for everyone and especially if you are a consultant. While many consultants tend to establish a consistent stream of work and income, there are no guarantees. However, there are also no guarantees in full-time employment either. While traditional employees do earn a consistent income, companies can eliminate their roles at any time, with or without severance.

Q. My client is pressuring me to become an employee and I want to remain a consultant. How can I continue to serve my client but respectfully tell them that I want to remain a consultant and don't want to be an employee?

A. This one can be tricky. Some clients assume that every consultant is doing contract work with the hope of becoming a full-time employee for that organization. While that may be the case for some, most of the consultants I work with don't want to go back to being a full-time employee. First, thank your client for considering you. Share how flattered you are that they would want you to take that role. Then share why you choose to be a consultant and how much you value supporting them in your current capacity. Emphasize the benefits to the client of having you work for them externally. As a consultant you are freed up to focus on the work, be productive, and get the work done that they want.

Q. How much time should I expect to be without work in between projects?

A. The short answer is that it depends. One of the most important things to get used to being a consultant is that it can be unpredictable when projects will come your way. You can increase your odds by constantly planting seeds. Sometimes you get to choose the work because you have a lot of options at once and other times you must actively search for projects. Remember, you get to decide when you want to take a break between projects, too. If you want consistent work, it's important to continuously implement the activities outlined in Chapter 6. If you are actively looking for work, consider offering your skills to a nonprofit for free or reduced fee. It's the right thing to do, it will expand your network, and it's a great way to show that you are working in your area of expertise.

Q. What if I can't find a contract?

A. See Chapter 6 for actionable guidance on how to land a contract. Stay focused on your daily activities, maintain a positive mindset, and plant those seeds!

Q. What if I end up on a project with a client where I know I will not be successful? What is the best way to gracefully walk away or manage through it so that I don't negatively impact my reputation?

A. Projects can start one way and then morph into something completely different. It's stressful to both the client and consultant and can lead to unrealistic expectations and a negative brand perception. It is your responsibility to manage communication with your client and regularly set clear expectations to avoid a difficult scenario. Ask the client the two critical questions often: "What do you value that I am doing?" and "What more can I do?" These are nonthreatening questions that can open positive dialogue with your client to steer you back on the path of success. Conversely, you may determine that the work is no longer in alignment with your brand and recommend winding down the project and professionally transition or end it.

Q. How do I manage not feeling part of the team I'm working with?

A. You're not alone. Many consultants feel that they are on the outside and not a member of the team. I invite you to reframe this mindset. Remember why you chose consulting in the first place. Maybe it was because you wanted a flexible schedule and didn't want to manage all the bureaucratic activities involved with being an employee. Perhaps you have other interests, kids or appreciate time for other activities. Focus on the benefits of your situation, rather than the downsides. And if you really want to be a part of a team again, then maybe it's time to consider transitioning to full-time employment. Revisit the pros and cons of consulting in Chapter 2 to help you determine the right situation for yourself at any given time in your career.

Q. I am so tired of hearing that budgets are tight. How do I get clients to see my value?

A. Budgets are a reality of any consultant's life, and it's on you to prove your value every day to justify your rate. Refer to the Rock Star Rules in Chapter 8, Deliver Excellence, for tips on how to showcase your value every day.

Q. How do I convince a client that while my résumé and background may indicate that I am overqualified for the project, THIS is the work I really want to do, right now, as a consultant?

A. Life is a marathon, not a sprint. Sometimes you just want to do work that's easy for you. This often happens to professionals who have been executives or senior leaders. That's okay. This is your opportunity to redefine your personal brand and explain why you want to do work that may be easy for you. Share your why with the client, even if it's for work and life flexibility, and stress that though the work may be second nature for you, you will make them look great!

Q.   How competitive is the consulting job market? What is the best way for me to stand out from the crowd?

A.   That is one of the main reasons I wrote this book! To help you stand out. Consulting is a crowded field, so clearly defining and sharing your personal brand is critical to your success. You must stand out in the sea of many and showcase your uniqueness. See Chapter 3 for how to build and develop your personal brand. Refer to these questions often. Stay true to your strengths and passions.

APPENDIX 2

RECOMMENDED READING

Brené Brown, *Daring Greatly: How the Courage to Be Vulnerable Transforms the Way We Live, Love, Parent, and Lead* (New York: Gotham Books, 2012).

Bill Burnett and Dave Evans, *Designing Your Life: How to Build a Well-Lived, Joyful Life* (New York: Knopf, 2016).

Dale Carnegie, *How to Win Friends & Influence People* (New York: Simon & Schuster, 1936).

Stephen R. Covey, *7 Habits of Highly Effective People* (New York: Free Press, 1989).

Paul Estes, *Gig Mindset: Reclaim Your Time, Reinvent Your Career, and Ride the Next Wave of Disruption* (Austin, Texas: Lioncrest Publishing, 2020).

Lisa Hufford, *Navigating the Talent Shift: How to Build On-Demand Teams that Drive Innovation, Control Costs, and Get Results* (New York: Springer Publishing, 2016).

Greg McKeown, *Essentialism: The Disciplined Pursuit of Less* (New York: Currency, 2014).

Daniel H. Pink, *Drive: The Surprising Truth About What Motivates Us* (New York: Riverhead Books, 2009).

ENDNOTES

Introduction

1. Visit https://www.simplicityci.com to learn more about the SPEED™ talent strategy.
2. Aaron Hurst and Dr. Anna Tavis, 2015 Workforce Purpose Index (New York: New York University and Imperative, 2015), https://cdn.imperative.com/media/public/Purpose_Index_2015.
3. Daniel H. Pink, *Drive: The Surprising Truth About What Motivates Us* (New York: Riverhead Books, 2011).

Chapter 1

1. Alex Sixt, "4 Trends That Are Shaping the Future of Work," *Entrepreneur*, July 28, 2020, https://www.entrepreneur.com/article/353861.
2. Karl Thompson, "What Percentage of Your Life Will You Spend at Work?" ReviseSociology, August 16, 2016, https://revisesociology.com/2016/08/16/percentage-life-work/.
3. Jeff Schwartz, Heather Stockton, and Dr. Kelly Monahan, *Forces of change: The Future of Work* (New York: Deloitte Insights, 2017), p. 2, https://www2.deloitte.com/content/dam/insights/us/articles/4322_Forces-of-change_FoW/DI_Forces-of-change_FoW.pdf.
4. Upwork, *Future Workforce Report*, 2020, https://www.upwork.com/i/future-workforce/fw/2020/.
5. Ibid.
6. Toptal Enterprise, *State Of The Workforce*, https://bs-uploads.toptal.io/blackfish-uploads/gated_content_article_page/content/attachment_file/attachment/2097/Toptal_-_State_of_the_Workforce-27ddc78ae2a23500ca4b353d153c235e.pdf.
7. U.S. Bureau of Labor Statistics, "Employee Tenure Summary," September 20, 2018, https://www.bls.gov/news.release/tenure.nr0.htm.
8. LinkedIn Talent Solutions, "Global Recruiting Trends 2017," https://www.slideshare.net/pedrooolito/linkedin-global-recruiting-trends-report-2017.
9. Erik Stettler, "The Power of Optionality, Part 1: Tech & Talent," Staffing.com, Toptal, March 11, 2020, https://www.staffing.com/the-power-of-optionality-part-1-tech-talent/.
10. Jack Altman, "How Much Does Employee Turnover Really Cost?" *HuffPost*, January 18, 2017, https://www.huffingtonpost.com/entry/how-much-does-employee-turnover-really-cost_us_587fbaf9e4b0474ad4874fb7.

11. Jason Albanese, "Four Ways Millennials Are Transforming Leadership," *Inc.*, Nov. 14, 2018, https://www.inc.com/jason-albanese/four-ways-millennials-are-transforming -leadership.html?cid=search.

12. Todd Bishop, "Microsoft posts $35B in revenue, up 15%, sees 'minimal net impact' from COVID-19 in quarter," GeekWire, April 29, 2020, https://www.geekwire.com /2020/microsoft-posts-35b-revenue-15-sees-minimal-net-impact-covid-19-quarter/.

13. John Healy, "How Consumer Expectations Are Driving The Future of Work," Staffing .com, Toptal, November 4, 2019, https://www.staffing.com/employee-centric-future -work/.

14. Susan Lund, Kweilin Ellingrud, Bryan Hancock, and James Manyika, "COVID-19 and jobs: Monitoring the US impact on people and places," McKinsey Global Institute, April 29, 2020, https://www.mckinsey.com/industries/public-sector/our-insights/covid-19 -and-jobs-monitoring-the-us-impact-on-people-and-places.

15. Jorge L. Ortiz, "'It's Nothing but Pain': The Latest on the Cases of Violence Against Black People that Sparked America's Racial Reckoning," *USA Today*, September 9, 2020, https://www.usatoday.com/story/news/nation/2020/09/09/george-floyd-breonna -taylor-jacob-blake-what-we-know/5753696002/.

16. Upwork, *Future Workforce Report*, 2020, https://www.upwork.com/i/future-workforce /fw/2020/.

Chapter 2

1. Greg McKeown, *Essentialism: The Disciplined Pursuit of Less* (New York: Crown Business, 2014), p. 235. Also in his 2012 blog for Harvard Business Review, https://hbr .org/2012/06/how-to-say-no-to-a-controlling.

2. Susan Lund, Kweilin Ellingrud, Bryan Hancock, and James Manyika, "COVID-19 and jobs: Monitoring the US impact on people and places," McKinsey Global Institute, April 29, 2020, https://www.mckinsey.com/industries/public-sector/our-insights/covid-19 -and-jobs-monitoring-the-us-impact-on-people-and-places.

3. Gina Hadley, "The Second Shift: Why On-demand Talent Advances Women," Staffing. com, Toptal, December 24, 2019, https://www.staffing.com/the-second-shift-why-on -demand-talent-advances-women/.

4. Kaytie Zimmerman, "Here's How Employers Can Prevent Their Employees From Job Hopping," *Forbes*, May 5, 2019, https://www.forbes.com/sites/kaytiezimmerman /2019/05/05/heres-how-employers-can-prevent-their-employees-from-job-hopping /#45e55af4b93c.

5. Upwork and Freelancers Union, *Freelancing in American 2018*, 5th Annual Report, https://www.upwork.com/i/freelancing-in-america/2018/.

6. Mary Oliver, "The Summer Day," *Devotions: Selected Poems of Mary Oliver* (New York: Penguin Publishing, 2017), p. 316.

Chapter 3

1. Lisa Hufford, "Personal Brand Playbook," https://info.simplicityci.com/download -the-personal-brand-playbook-lisa-hufford.

2. Brené Brown, "Listening to shame," TED2012, March 2012, https://www.ted.com /talks/brene_brown_listening_to_shame.

3. Seth Godin, Seth's Blog, https://seths.blog/2016/12/the-best-way-to-stand-for-something/.

4. Jeff Beer, "One Year Later, What Did We Learn from Nike's Blockbuster Colin Kaepernick Ad?" *Fast Company*, September 5, 2019, https://www.fastcompany.com/90399316/one-year-later-what-did-we-learn-from-nikes-blockbuster-colin-kaepernick-ad.

5. Mary Papenfuss, "Nike's Controversial Colin Kaepernick Ad Wins Emmy For Best Commercial," *HuffPost*, September 16, 2019, https://www.huffpost.com/entry/colin-kaepernick-donald-trump-nike-ad-creative-arts-emmy_n_5d7efe19e4b00d69059b023f.

6. In the November 25, 2011, issue of the *New York Times*, Patagonia ran an ad declaring "Don't Buy This Jacket" and invited readers to take the Common Threads Initiative pledge to reduce, repair, reuse, recycle, and reimagine, https://www.patagonia.com/stories/dont-buy-this-jacket-black-friday-and-the-new-york-times/story-18615.html.

7. Rose Marcario, CEO of Patagonia, "Why I'm Joining the People's Climate March," inviting participation in the September 21, 2020, Climate March in New York, https://www.patagonia.com/stories/why-im-joining-the-peoples-climate-march/story-17899.html.

8. John Blake, "He was MLK's mentor, and his meeting Gandhi changed history. But Howard Thurman was largely unknown, until now," CNN, February 1, 2019, https://www.cnn.com/2019/02/01/us/howard-thurman-mlk-gandhi/index.html.

9. Marianne Williamson, *A Return to Love: A Reflection on the Principles of "A Course in Miracles"* (New York: HarperCollins, 1992), p. 164.

Chapter 4

1. Steve Jobs, "'You've got to find what you love,' Jobs says," commencement address at Stanford University, June 12, 2005, video and text available at https://news.stanford.edu/2005/06/14/jobs-061505/.

2. Upwork, *Future Workforce Report*, 2020, https://www.upwork.com/i/future-workforce/fw/2020/.

Chapter 5

1. Jen Hubley Luckwaldt, "Gut Check: Why Are Women Uncomfortable Talking About Salary?" PayScale, 2016, https://www.payscale.com/salary-negotiation-guide/why-women-are-uncomfortable-talking-about-salary.

2. Randstad, "Salary and compensation statistics on the impact of COVID-19," survey conducted June 22–25, 2020, https://rlc.randstadusa.com/for-business/learning-center/future-workplace-trends/randstad-compensation-insights-1.

Chapter 6

1. Maddy Osman, "Mind-Blowing LinkedIn Statistics and Facts (2020)," Kinsta.com, April 10, 2020, https://kinsta.com/blog/linkedin-statistics/.

2. Lydia Abbot, "10 Tips for Picking the Right LinkedIn Profile Picture," LinkedIn, August 5, 2019, https://business.linkedin.com/talent-solutions/blog/2014/12/5-tips-for-picking-the-right-linkedin-profile-picture.

3. Stephanie Chacharon, "Better together: 5 takeaways from TalentConnect 2019," Point of View, Simplicity Consulting, September 29, 2019, https://blog.simplicityci.com/better-together-linkedin-talent-connect-5-takeaways.

4. Aimee Groth, "You're the Average of the Five People You Spend the Most Time With," *Business Insider*, July 24, 2012, https://www.businessinsider.com/jim-rohn-youre-the-average-of-the-five-people-you-spend-the-most-time-with-2012-7.
5. Alyssa, "Are Social Media and Depression Linked? Why?" Behavioral Health of the Palm Beaches, May 16, 2020, https://www.bhpalmbeach.com/are-depression-and-social-media-usage-linked/.

Chapter 7

1. Stephen R. Covey, "Habit 2: Begin with the End in Mind," Genius.com, https://genius.com/Stephen-r-covey-habit-2-begin-with-the-end-in-mind-annotated.
2. Bruce Horovitz, "CEO: Under Armour will get 'bigger, better,'" *USA Today*, February 21, 2014, https://www.usatoday.com/story/money/business/2014/02/21/under-armour-winter-olympics-sochi-speedskating/5652457/.

Chapter 9

1. In his book *7 Habits of Highly Effective People* (New York: Free Press, 1989), Stephen R. Covey lists number seven as "Sharpen the saw," which he describes as the preservation and enhancement of oneself. This quote is found at https://www.franklincovey.com/the-7-habits/habit-7.html.
2. Tony Woodall, "QOD-031: Arianna Huffington—Failure is not the opposite of success, it's part of success," Goal Getting Podcast, July 31, 2015 (includes recording), http://www.goalgettingpodcast.com/qod31/.
3. Lindsay Holmes, "Self-Care For Women Is More Work Than Buying Products," *HuffPost*, March 11, 2019, https://www.huffpost.com/entry/women-self-care_l_5c48d765e4b0b6693676728d.

Conclusion

1. Lynn Okura, "The Most Important Lesson Maya Angelou Learned From Her Grandmother (VIDEO)," *HuffPost*, May 30, 2014, https://www.huffpost.com/entry/maya-angelou-master-class_n_5420108.

INDEX

About the Author

LISA HUFFORD is founder and CEO of Simplicity Consulting, the innovative enterprise marketing services consultancy that helps companies like Microsoft, Amazon, and Providence accelerate sales and operationalize their business at speed and scale by accessing experts on demand. Founded in 2006, Simplicity's mission is to help everyone thrive in the new world of work. Recognition includes five years as an Inc. 5000 fastest-growing private company in America and one of *Puget Sound Business Journal*'s largest woman-owned businesses in Washington state.

Lisa has been named an Inc. Top 10 Female Entrepreneur and selected as an Ernst & Young Entrepreneurial Winning Woman. She's a champion for professionals transitioning to consulting and advises companies on building flexible, project-based teams that add immediate value, as discussed in her three books:

- *Work, Your Way: Reinvent yourself, Create the Life You Want, and Thrive As a Consultant*
- *Navigating the Talent Shift: How to Build On-Demand Teams That Drive Innovation, Control Costs, and Get Results*
- *Personal Brand Playbook*

www.lisahufford.com • www.simplicityci.com
https://www.linkedin.com/in/lisahufford/
@lisahufford